A Passion for Life
Using the Power Within to Drive Your Success

John Wiley & Sons Canada, Ltd.

National Library of Canada Cataloguing in Publication Data

A passion for life : using the power within to drive your
success / The Power Within.

ISBN-13 978-0-470-83782-5
ISBN-10 0-470-83782-9

1. Success. 2. Self-actualization (Psychology). I. Power Within (Firm)

BF637.S8P375 2006   158.1   C2006-900479-X

Production Credits:
Cover design: Art Silveira
Interior text design: Adrian So
Typesetting: Mike Chan

Printer: Tri-Graphic Printing Ltd.

John Wiley & Sons Canada, Ltd.
6045 Freemont Blvd.
Mississauga, Ontario
L5R 4J3

Printed in Canada

1 2 3 4 5 TRI 10 09 08 07 06

TABLE OF CONTENTS

introduction

There exists a quality of character within the men and women of high achievement that separates them from the masses. This quality can infuse us with an enthusiasm that deters fatigue, a courage that emboldens our spirit, and a joyous sense of adventure for the life we have been blessed to captain. With this quality of character, we have the internal fortitude to build kingdoms; without it, we are hostage to our fears and weaknesses.

People may be born to privilege—and fail. Born to talent—and flounder. Given opportunity—and squander it. They may achieve material success, but without this precious quality their life will seem empty and hollow. What is this mysterious quality? It is married to every great enthusiasm, intertwined with our deepest desires. It goes hand in hand with every dream, every great love that we harbor, whether for a person, a business idea, or a cause that consumes our hearts and minds. It will carry us through our darkest moments, and lead us to our greatest victories. It is the defining quality that separates the good from the very best.

This quality is *passion*.

You have seen men and women who should have been overwhelmed by circumstance—and were not. Passion carried them through. You have seen companies threatened with bankruptcy, and the owner refused to concede defeat. Passion served as his armor. You have seen marriages threatened by illness, financial ruin, or self-destruction—and yet they prevailed. Passion was the couple's counselor. You have seen mothers and fathers lose their children to accident, sickness or violence—and rebound with vigor. Passion fueled their cause to find meaning in their loss and to take action to save others. Passion makes the difference in all of our pursuits, in each arena of our lives.

At The Power Within, we believe in living a life of passion. This book is a call to arms to every man and woman who believes as we do: life is meant to be lived fully and it is our privilege and responsibility to engage our talents and pursue those things that we hold dear. We each have the ability to create the life we desire.

As you are pursuing your dreams, we invite you to return to the words and ideas in the coming pages to remind you of the powers that already reside within your spirit, powers yet to be fully unleashed. We invite you to share your passion with the world.

You Already Have the Tools

It is not uncommon for high achievers to excel in one or more key areas of their life, while struggling to achieve success in others. This is to be expected. But you do not have to be confined by what defines others and what is considered "average." You are not average. You know it by the simple fact that you are reading this work. Exceptional people invest time and energy in self-discovery and self-mastery, and the average person does not. It is true that success has or will come to you more easily in some areas than others, but with work, you can enjoy victory in every area of your life.

You already have the mark of success. There is something that defines and makes you remarkable. You have a genius in some area of your life. You have enjoyed victory in some endeavor. It can be as grand as building a $100-million company with your creativity, leadership and work, or as subtle as soothing the tension in a small home with your grace and good humor. It is also possible that you harbor a more rigid definition of success that only includes material wealth and career advancement; but success can be seen in a variety of hues, and we can create a multi-colored masterpiece of our lives.

You may have felt resigned to enjoying success in only one area of your life, having struggled to make positive changes before. You may have committed to your spouse that you would be home on time for dinner from now on, but your passion for work draws you like an inescapable magnet to stay late. You may have promised to make a change in your career and pursue something more in line with your interests and abilities, but your passion to be there for your kids after school leaves you feeling conflicted. In the past, translating success from one area into other areas in your life may have eluded you. If we've tried and failed before, what else can you do?

You have previously mastered many of the principles of success. You already know how to build a company, a marriage, a home, your portfolio, your body, or your volunteer cause. The same principles of success are transferable directly into other areas of your life, with passion as the catalyst. Passion is the missing ingredient. You need only to find the passion to further identify these principles and utilize them; then you will reap the rewards of the life you desire.

What is Passion?

What is most beautiful and sacred to you? What would you feel incomplete without? When you have identified that which brings you complete joy, your own unquenchable desire to achieve that goal will become your passion—the inner drive that turns your dreams into a shining reality.— Author unknown

Passion is the internal experience and outward expression of our greatest possible love and enthusiasm. It fills us with focus, energy and determination. It is the fuel that allows us to complete the supreme journey. It is the fulcrum against which the largest mountains can be moved. It is the springboard from which all of our greatest accomplishments are launched. Passion is a deep love for something, whether a person, idea, company or cause. It is a love so intense, so consuming that it eradicates the normal barriers that may arise in our pursuits. Any obstacle that stumbles before the light of our true passion will soon face its demise.

Passion is evident in your thoughts, words and actions. It is revealed in your desire to accomplish a goal that is deeply rewarding. It is expressed through your resolve to finish what you have started, the spark in your eye from great excitement, the spring in your step from boundless energy, the magnetism in your words as you visualize the completion of your dreams and the conviction in your voice as you say, "I mean to accomplish this!"

With passion, all doors will eventually open before you; the gatekeepers on the other side will eventually tire. Passion is the fire that allows the hare to outlast the wolf. The wolf is running to catch his dinner, while the hare is running for his life. As long as your deepest passion is at the forefront of your mind, you will succeed in your endeavors. It cannot be a passing fancy, a mild interest, or even a strong concern: your passion must dominate your thoughts, govern every action and haunt you in your dreams.

When all of your thoughts, words and deeds are fully aligned with your mission, you are infused with an unquenchable energy. You erase from your mind any thoughts of sorrow, betrayal, sadness or loss. Instead, your thoughts are dominated with images of hope, victory and celebration. To live a life of passion means that you have embarked on a quest to fully satisfy your highest ambitions. It means that you will do so with a joyous and grateful spirit, and greet each day with vigor. Passion promises that you will be unstoppable.

Inject Passion into Everything You Do

Every great and commanding moment in the annals of the world is the triumph of some enthusiasm.
—Ralph Waldo Emerson

It comes down to this: you must make the decision to be passionate. How did you become passionate in other areas of your life? Ask yourself: "What makes me passionate about something?"

Perhaps you're passionate about something because it meets your values or touches on your ultimate sense of purpose. Or perhaps you chose to focus on the positive aspects that you love about this thing, or it stirs emotions like courage, allowing you to easily vault over challenges. Or maybe it allows you to connect with people whom you love, or it opens the doorway for greater prosperity, allowing you a rewarding and enjoyable lifestyle. Or possibly it gives you the chance to create something greater than you, something that will touch other people's lives. This is the recipe for every great sustainable success. In this book, we will take each of those components and study them in depth, so that you may apply them across the board in all of your pursuits.

We will help you create greater passion in every area of your life by:

- **Setting goals.** Our goals embrace our highest values and fill us with a sense of mission. They serve to inspire the best within us, for the act of naming what matters most to us is an act of great courage. By identifying what we love most, we are implicitly asserting that we will design our lives around our greatest dreams. In setting goals, we stand ready to marshal our full talents and energies to achieve our dreams.
- **Mastering our emotions.** We will use the tool of our positive energies as a shield against our pessimism, fears and procrastination. In doing so, we will see the blessing in each challenge, use courage to defeat our enemies, both real and imagined, and mobilize our resources when fatigue saps our minds and bodies.
- **Enhancing our relationships.** This means nurturing the greatest treasure available to us: the people we love. We recognize that in order to achieve our greatest dreams, we will require the help of others. We accept that help with a grateful heart and resolve to encourage the best within people by recognizing their inherent strengths and mastering the secrets of human interaction.
- **Deciphering the code of financial mastery.** We realize that if our goals require material resources in order to achieve them, we must become students of wealth creation. We see

that the pathway to material success lies in our beliefs about money, and we resolve to dissolve the mental barriers that may have held us back from achieving our true potential.

- **Permitting ourselves to enjoy balance.** A passionate life is a life to be enjoyed—one in which we stop along the journey to celebrate our victories. We recognize that passion can fuel our body only so far before we must become effective stewards of our health in mind, body and spirit and that the sustained pursuit of our dreams requires regular renewal to recharge our batteries.
- **Finding a greater purpose in our lives through making a contribution to others**. Sometimes the greatest enthusiasm springs from the pleasure we receive in setting goals that benefit more than just ourselves, in parenting a child with integrity, using our personal setbacks as a platform to serve the community, or standing up for those who cannot defend themselves. By giving to others, we may discover the ultimate source of unrelenting energy to fuel our performance.

This book is about making a decision to live a passionate life. In the pursuit of your highest ideals, you will find that passion can be injected into everything you do. As we spend these next few hours and days together, you will remind yourself of the principles of success that have thus far contributed to growth in some areas of your life. Now, you will revisit these principles with a new eye, looking to see how you may apply them more completely in every area of your life experience.

Let's begin.

1 master goal setting

In the field of personal development, one of the few things that can be empirically validated is that individuals and organizations that set goals accomplish more.
—Steven Covey, *First Things First*[1]

It is a familiar scene: the clock approaches midnight on New Year's Eve and people around the globe have gathered together to celebrate the moment with festivities, good cheer and merriment. As the clock strikes 12 midnight and the crowd roars with applause, you may pause to consider what the last year has brought and what you have to look forward to in the coming year. You may consider the victories you have enjoyed and the defeats you have endured; the relationships built and the friendships that have faded; the lessons learned and the lessons lost. Perhaps you begin to look forward to the New Year with a sense of positive hope and expectation, believing that the best is yet to come. You feel a sense of invigoration as you participate in the popular activity of setting New Year's resolutions. You may say to yourself, "This is the year I'm finally going to lose that weight and get in shape! I'm making the decision to quit smoking! I'm

1 Stephen R., Covey *First Things First*. New York: Free Press/Simon & Shuster, 1994, p. 324.

going to get serious about my financial future! I'm finally going to launch that business venture! I'm going to pursue that creative dream! I'm going to live the life I truly desire!"

Sadly, as the coming weeks unfold, many people find that those initial resolutions fall by the wayside as "real life" sets in: the unforeseen obstacles, the distractions, the loss of enthusiasm needed to press through and achieve the goals that we have set out for ourselves. Journalists debate the merits of setting resolutions at all, and the most pessimistic say that we shouldn't bother, because most people will fall victim to inertia, lose momentum, run out of steam and simply give in to their weaknesses in the end. "Why bother trying?" they proclaim, "when I'm just going to quit anyway?"

Leaders are deaf to these negative proclamations. While the common man or woman allows circumstance to buffet them around like a leaf in the breeze, exceptional individuals have an internal fortitude to press on and achieve the prize they seek. They affix their gaze upon a specific target and pursue it with ferocity. The endurance required to attain a long-term result is born from the deep love they have for their life and the people that they are leading, whether their family, their employees or their community. Leaders have an overriding sense of purpose that spurs them to action when fatigue and distraction threaten their resolve. This sense of purpose, this fire within, stems from their passion to achieve the goal at hand.

Champions set and achieve goals. It is nearly impossible to enjoy an intensely rewarding and meaningful life without designing it according to your deepest desires and values. Exceptional lives are not an accident; individuals are not called to do great work because they had nothing more interesting to do. They design, build and bring to market their great works out of their *deepest* interests, out of a wellspring of enthusiasm for their calling. But all great works, indeed all great lives, are lived on purpose, with a clear plan and design. You are fully capable of living the life you desire, but only if you first decide to do so. Achieving your dreams is presupposed by knowing what your dreams are—and having a plan to make them a reality.

Challenges of Goal Setting

While unfortunate, it is not uncommon for many people to struggle with setting goals effectively. We also face great challenges with following through and accomplishing them. There can be several reasons for this, but some of the greatest obstacles to effective goal setting may be the *mental* or *psychological* barriers that we confront. Our external foes are not nearly as debilitating as the internal enemies called "doubt," "indecision," and "fear"; our greatest threat to success comes from *ourselves*. Throughout the rest of this chapter, we will be speaking extensively on how to set goals, but first let's turn our attention to some of the common mental challenges that people face while setting goals. The four most common examples are:

- I don't know why I need to set goals.
- I don't know how to set goals.
- I don't know what goals to set.
- I'm afraid.

Why Set Goals?

The race for excellence knows no finish line.—Anonymous

What determines the fate of *average* men and women? The answer includes many things: circumstance, indecision, fear, conflicting desires and social pressure. What determines the fate of *great* men and women? The answer is: *they do.* And they first do it by setting goals.

Goals are the premier tool of excellence. They spur you into action when lethargy beckons. They fill you with power and motivate you internally, leaving the people around you to wonder with curiosity why you always seem to be bursting with energy. Goals enable you to become the person you were meant to be, according to your ultimate vision. They insist that you overcome your weaknesses and improve yourself constantly. They are the antithesis of apathy, since you deeply care about your actions and their outcome. Goals enhance your decision-making process; you are never confused about major choices when the overall objective is clear. They drive away boredom, since you have embarked on a passionate quest. They allow you to create your future in advance and breathe a sense of certainty into your day. They harness the full power of your talents and energies and focus those energies upon a single point of interest, allowing your drive to burn through obstacles much like a laser beam burns a hole through metal. Light that is diffused over a wide area merely creates warmth. Light that is concentrated into a pinpoint will cut through the obstacle to its target.

Belief in the process of setting goals springs first from the belief that you can control much of the course of your life and your future. Why set goals? Because in setting goals you are consciously saying, "I decide my fate, not others. I am the author of my destiny. I won't rely on providence to shine upon me and bless me with fortune; I choose to bless myself through my own ingenuity and industry." Is it possible that your plans will be laid to waste? *Yes.* Is it possible that disaster may befall you and you suffer catastrophic heartbreak? *Yes.* Is it possible that your efforts, however well intentioned, will prove fruitless? *Yes.* But the common man or woman hides behind the fear of potential disappointment, not realizing that the greatest disappointment awaits them in the twilight of their life if they choose to risk nothing! The uncommon achiever takes the calculated risk and proclaims to the world, "This is the thing that I will do." Your character and bravery are crystallized when you stake your word on your effort and achievement. Will you do the thing that you have promised? Cowards shrink from commitment; heroes embrace it.

You are capable of heroic acts. You are capable of great things. It only remains for you to do them. You may feel this burgeoning desire to take action, to sit up, to lean forward, to leap from your chair and take hold of everything you want from your life, to shape your course with the strength of your mind and will. You deserve everything you are willing to work for. You deserve the greatness that your life can become. Why set goals? Because someone is going to decide the life that you lead. Either you will decide by conscious choice, or the world around you will decide by default. If other people are making decisions for your life, they are likely making the decisions that offer them the greatest benefit.

Why set goals? Because your life is too precious not to!

But I Don't Know How to Set Goals

The second most common reason people don't set goals is that they are inexperienced or unskilled in doing so. Sadly, one of the most important skills that can ever be developed is not only absent from the school curriculum, but is deliberately and obviously removed from the decision-making opportunities that many young children face. From early childhood, most people have their goals set for them by well-meaning parents and authority figures through their developing years. They are told, "Do well in grade school so that you are prepared for high school. Do well in high school so that you gain admittance to university. Do well in university so that you can get a good job ..." But when the time finally comes to set the first major goal for themselves, for example, to decide which course of study to take and which career to pursue, young people find themselves woefully unprepared to make a decision and seemingly cast their future in stone. Clarity of purpose has eluded them, because they were never forced to flex their decision-making muscles. When asked, "Why are you in school?" the final answer usually boils down to "because I was told to."

Consider how many college and university students arrive on campus with no clear purpose or idea of what they want to do with their lives. And when they finish their education, many of those who do know what they want waver on their focus to accomplish the goal on which they have invested years of study and tens of thousands of dollars in training. How many people do you know with university degrees that have nothing to do with their career? Too often students leave school and latch on to the first job available in order to pay the rent, and student loans. Often, 15 years slips by before they wake up to realize what has happened.

It is entirely possible that you have a keen desire to achieve a goal in a certain area, yet you have been frustrated with repeated failure. Success in this one endeavor has eluded you. Doubly frustrating is the fact that you truly want what you are after, and you may feel like you have applied every positive principle to its acquisition. But goal setting and goal achieving are learned skills, and without repeated usage, the psychological muscle required to set goals will wither and atrophy. Sometimes, we are so close to the problem that we cannot see the step in the process that we are leaving out. Whenever Tiger Woods plays, he is always interested in the consultation and assistance of his caddy; this way, he has two pairs of eyes on his game instead of just one.

You may believe that you are following all of the principles of success, but if you are only taking your own counsel and advice, you may not be able to see for yourself which critical step you may have neglected.

But I Don't Know What Goals to Set

The third reason that people may not set goals is that they are unsure of what goal they should set. Perhaps you have already been afflicted with this challenge. Consider this: How did you choose the goals that are currently directing your schedule and energies? How did you decide that these goals are the most important things to pursue? With great regret, many so-called "successful" people discover too late that the arenas they have conquered were not the most important things to them, and they are left feeling empty and disillusioned with this realization. It is of no long-term value to fight your way up the ladder, only to discover later on that the ladder you are climbing has been leaning against the wrong building. If success in one area of your life means disaster in another, will the success still be as sweet? Will you look back and feel that the sacrifice was worth the effort (which it may have been), or will you look back and wish that you had chosen a different course? How do you avoid reaching a crossroads in later years where you regret a goal that you have set for yourself?

Many times, people will set and achieve goals and enjoy great success, but for the wrong reasons. Perhaps you are living out someone else's dreams instead of your own. Perhaps your parents dearly hoped that you would become a surgeon. And so, without even consciously realizing why you were doing it, you adopted their dreams and goals and found yourself with a busy practice. You are respected by your friends, you enjoy a comfortable material lifestyle and, most of all, your parents are incredibly proud. But one day you wake up and realize that your deepest passion is something else entirely. Perhaps you felt called to the ministry and had truly wanted to be a pastor, to share your religious convictions with others. You set and achieved goals, but perhaps not the right ones for you.

Maybe you've become a partner in a law firm. You enjoy prestige, money, power, but you feel that something is missing. Deep inside, you feel called to make a more significant impact in people's lives. Certainly, your clients appreciate you and you do excellent work to serve them, but secretly your desire is to teach children, to share with them how they can conquer their fears and make themselves into anything they want. You have set the goal of becoming a partner, and you have achieved your goal. But you aren't leading by example, because you aren't doing what you really want.

Perhaps you've become an accountant. Your family is safe and secure, and your finances are in perfect health. As long as you don't do anything risky or foolish, a comfortable retirement is assured for you and your loved ones. You have set the goal and accomplished it. But secretly, you yearn for adventure. You want to take the big risk, to test your mettle and see what you're really made of. You are brimming with business ideas, constantly seeing opportunities where others do not, and you know that you could pull it off and build a company of your own. But you aren't sure; aren't you supposed to play it safe? Isn't that what responsible people do?

But I'm Afraid to Set Goals

The fourth reason that people may not set goals is that they are paralyzed by fear. This is the silent killer of success. When people over 90 years of age are asked, "What do you regret the most?" they reply almost unanimously, "I regret what I *didn't* do!" It is not usually our mistakes that cause the deepest feelings of loss, but the times that fear won the battle over courage and we didn't act.

What is the source of our fear? **Many times, we may fear failure**. We will play a tape recorder of negativity over and over in our mind, making defeatist statements to ourselves and asking our subconscious negative questions: "What if it doesn't work? What if I make a mistake? What if I look foolish? What will people say about me if I drop the ball on this? How will I face my family and friends if I've bragged about success, only to fail? How embarrassed will I feel? How can I ever look myself in the mirror again? How can I stand to fail again?" Negative thinking will ensure that you become a magnet for negative results. Perhaps the pain of failure is too great if you have a competitive spirit; perhaps it will mean that you feel embarrassed or sad. Perhaps you've been crushed with disappointment and can't bear to endure pain that great again.

You may fear the unknown. The uncertainty of the next moment shakes you to the core. Most people succumb to a mediocre life because the stability of routine is intoxicating. Whether remaining in an unfulfilling relationship because things are "okay," remaining in an unfulfilling job because you can count on a paycheck, or shying away from your life's dream because trying might mean that you discover that you don't have what it takes after all, most people would rather fend off the demon they know than the demon they don't. But life's rewards don't go to the people that shy away from their deepest convictions and desires; in fact as Robert F. Kennedy said, "Only those who dare to fail greatly can ever achieve greatly."

You may fear success. What will be expected of you if you truly make it big? Will you have to keep up a tremendous work schedule? Will more people count on you and depend upon your decisiveness in critical moments? Will your enemies be watching your performance and hoping you trip up? Will your friends and family feel uncomfortable around you if you are more successful than them? Were you raised to believe that it's wrong to be more successful than your parents? How can you be humble and spiritual if you have become successful? Will you worry if you are a "one-hit-wonder" and not have the chops to continue to be successful? Will people find out that they made a mistake to promote you and that you don't feel qualified inside?

These are all questions that can drive us to avoid the daring leap into greatness. If you catch yourself running any of these scripts in your mind, let the fire alarm go off in your head that warns of a negative, pessimistic attitude creeping in—and take action to douse your fears with confidence. There is only one way to douse the flames of fear, and that is through *taking action.*

Brainstorming Your Goals

By reading this book, you are taking action this moment; you are seeking something. Is it wisdom? Is it confirmation of your currently-held values and beliefs about success principles? Perhaps you are seeking motivation; the right combination of words that will light a fire within your soul to take action, to dare mightily, and to race forward with newfound enthusiasm for your greatest dreams. Maybe you are searching for something to become passionate about. Maybe you are searching for a cause to champion, a mission to pursue, a greater sense of purpose in your life. Perhaps you seek the catalyst to renew your relationships, your health, or any other area of your life.

The point is this: in order to get the life that you want, you need to clearly know: *what is it that you want?* You need to 'believe it' before you can 'see it'… you need to decide what your next step is: you need to have a goal. And it must be a goal that leaves you fantasizing about its attainment through the day, waking you from sleep in the morning, leaving you brimming with an unearthly energy that carries you into the night; it must be a goal that *fires your passion*.

Courage and imagination must sow the seeds of your life-long adventure, not fear and drudgery. The challenges to goal-setting that we have described earlier in this chapter may feel all-too-real to you; perhaps you've struggled with each one of them at some point. But today can be the day that you cast aside those impediments, whichever may remain. It is true that you may face uncertainty; you may face your lack of experience in setting goals; you may even face failure … but you must let none of these factors become a deterrent to you reaping the rewards of your talents. Your imagination must explode with ideas for what your life can become; your faith and self-assurance must grab hold of those ideas and breathe life into them. Your *future* reputation of success will be preceded by your *current* reputation for effective goal-setting.

John Goddard

John Goddard is legendary for setting and achieving goals. At the ripe age of 15, John sat down with a pad of paper and a pencil and asked himself a powerful question: "What would I like to do with my life?" That afternoon he began to brainstorm and capture his ideas. His imagination and scope of interest had no limits; he set goals in every conceivable sphere of interest. Some of his goals would be easily attained; some seemed nearly impossible. Some could be accomplished near home; some would require traveling the world. Some goals could be checked off the list that week; some would prove to take a lifetime of preparation.

John Goddard allowed no limits to his imagination and drafted an original set of 127 lifetime goals. Included on his list were goals such as exploring the Nile and Amazon rivers; climbing

Mount Everest; exploring the Great Barrier reef in Australia; visiting the North Pole, the Great Wall of China, Easter Island, the Taj Mahal and the Eiffel Tower; skin diving to 40 feet; skydiving; learning French and Spanish; reading the works of Shakespeare; composing music; marrying and having children.

Over the course of his lifetime, John has accomplished 109 of the 127 quests that he has set for himself. He says, **"To dare is to do . . . to fear is to fail."** John reasoned that since it was so normal to make a grocery list or a to-do list for our tasks of the day, wouldn't it also be natural and normal to write a list for what we want to accomplish in our lifetime?

Putting Pen to Paper

The next few moments will provide an illuminating insight into your ultimate destiny, for we will carry out one of the simplest and most profound exercises that a self-actualized person can undertake: the capturing of goals on paper. Writing goals allows you to create your future in advance. You deserve the greatest life experience possible, and this next exercise will open the doorway for you to design your life. This is an exciting moment, because you literally get to choose how your life story unfolds for yourself!

This may be a totally new experience for you. Or, if you have done an exercise similar to this in the past, this will be a positive refresher and this chapter will likely provide new insights and strategies to further enhance your goal-setting ability. Over the next few moments we will begin to refine your personal and professional goals. Settle yourself in a quiet area, free of distraction and discomfort. Relax, get comfortable and get ready to have a little fun!

It's important that as your creative juices begin to flow, you can quickly jot your ideas down without being interrupted. We encourage you to write down every goal that you have considered, regardless of whether or not it seems realistic right now.

Add as much detail as possible. *Don't worry right now about how you will accomplish the goals.* Write down goals for every area of your life. Write down goals that excite you to even see them on the page before you; goals that can take your breath away!

Robert Schuler said "What would you do if you knew you could not fail?" Set your goals with this mantra repeating over and over in your mind. Let your ideas spill out of your mind onto the page, with delirious enthusiasm. Pretend that you are a grown-up kid at Christmas, and everything you write down will come true! What would you do if you won the lottery? How much would you like to win? What would you do with it? Would you pursue a life's dream? Would you start a business, or enhance your existing career? Would you help your family? Purchase a new home? Go on a vacation; and if so, where? Start a charity? Retire early? Go back to school? Embark on a daring adventure? Brainstorm ideas for every area of your life: mind, body, spirit, career, finances and relationships. Consider the following questions to spur your creativity:

* What would you love to work on, if money was not a factor? What goals do you have for your career?
* What type of person would you like to become? What type of character would you like to be known by?
* What goals do you have for your health? What type of body and level of fitness would you like to enjoy? What body do you want to see in the mirror each day?
* What goals do you have for your relationships? Who is important to you in your life, and how can you give even more into that relationship? Which people would you like to attract into your life?
* What goals do you have for your finances? How much money would you like to earn? What would you like your net worth to be? How much savings would you like to have?

- Who would you help out financially? Family, friends, community?
- What is your dream lifestyle? Describe a "perfect day" from sunrise to sunset. What do you do? Where do you go? Who do you see?
- If you had enough money, what creative project has always been close to your heart that you would like to do?
- Have you ever been afraid to go after something because of financial limitations? What risks would you now take?
- What personal goals would you set? How would you like to improve yourself? How would you expand your mind and your skills?
- What charities would you like to contribute to? What volunteer work would you like to engage in if time and money had no limits? What causes have touched your heart?
- What would your home be like? Would it be custom designed? Would you live by the lake, the ocean, the forest, the suburbs, downtown? Would it be a mansion in an upscale community, a cottage with a private dock for your fishing boat, an urban castle, a condo overlooking the city lights at night?
- What toys would you like to have? Home theatre, sports car, jewelry or clothing, motor home, cottage, speedboat, or jet ski?
- Do you have any educational goals? Would you like to study something, simply because you'd enjoy it? Would you like to do research?
- What would make you feel profoundly disappointed if you didn't accomplish or experience this in your lifetime?
- What would you do if you knew you could not fail?

Keep writing as much and as fast as you can. Brainstorm ideas for every area of your life. Don't leave anything off the page, even if you're not sure how to attain the goal right now!

5 Steps to Accomplishment

Once we have recognized the value in setting goals, identified any possible psychological barriers, and brainstormed our goals without limitations, it is time to turn our attention to bringing our goals to life. HOW do we accomplish the goals we've set? What is the "formula" for success? Throughout the rest of this chapter, we will answer that exact question. We will cover in detail the specific strategies that the most successful goal-achievers use to claim their personal victories. To do this, you must go back through the goals you've brainstormed and apply the forthcoming strategies to each one. For the remainder of this chapter, we will get clear on which goals are the most important to us based upon our *value* systems and sense of *mission*. We will also refine these goals and ensure they are structured with the principles of successful *goal development*. Finally, we will create *action plans* for the attainment of our goals.

The principles of effective goal setting are as timeless as they are absolute. To neglect one of these principles in a misguided attempt to find a short-cut to success would result in wasting time unnecessarily, possible disappointment, or even failure. To follow these 5 Steps to Accomplishment will guarantee that you are abiding by the timeless principles of success, following in the footsteps of the greatest achievers of all time, and have every advantage directed towards your ultimate success. Once you have brainstormed your goals, the 5 Steps to Accomplishment are:

1. Visualize the end result.
2. Clarify your values.
3. Define your mission.
4. Reinforce your goals.
5. Develop your action plan.

1. Visualize the End Result

How do you want it to all turn out? In his masterpiece *7 Habits of Highly Effective People*, Steven Covey says that we must "Begin with the end in mind." He describes a funeral procession that you are sitting in on, three years from now. The mood is somber as you approach the casket to pay your respects, only to find yourself recoiling in horror as you realize that the person in the casket is *you*. You have died, and your loved ones have come to mourn your loss as you mysteriously look in on your own funeral. One by one, people from the various areas of your life offer a eulogy, celebrating your life. The question is: What would you like them to say about you, when you die? What do you hope that your spouse, children, friends, colleagues and community say about your time on Earth, your deeds and actions, your code of conduct, your mind and spirit? How will the final report on your life be read?

What if you wrote your memoirs today? What would be your greatest accomplishment? What would be the strongest area of your life? What would be your greatest regret? Your biggest missed opportunity? What would your life teach others? And if you had enough time, what would you like to add to your memoirs? What successes would you have yet to achieve?

This scenario offers an introspective opportunity. It challenges us to clarify our greatest dreams and values. What is the purpose of this exercise?

- To ensure that your ladder is leaning against the right wall. By visualizing the end result, you can fast-forward to the end of your saga and decide that the hero wins and saves the kingdom and his or her one true love in the process.
- To create your future in advance and protect yourself from the whispers of others that may cause you to lose your way, through honoring their wishes instead of your own.

- To clear your head of the fog created by the title on your business card, the size of your expense account, the envious looks of passersby as your drive past in your luxury sedan, if you are still not feeling satisfied in your core.

Don't set the goal of getting a promotion because it is the next step; set the goal of getting a promotion because it is exactly what you want for yourself. Don't set the goal of raising a million dollars for the charity you support through work because last year you raised $500,000 and the group has asked you to chair the committee again. Set the goal to serve because your heart is bursting with love for your cause. Don't just choose the *next* step on the path before you; choose the *right path.*

2. Clarify Your Values

Knowing which goals to set springs first from clarifying your value system. It will offer insight into your personal motivators and ensure that you will achieve success in the areas that will have the maximum impact in your life. To think about what you would want people to say about you at your own funeral may be a key in identifying your values. Ask yourself, "What are the driving forces in my life that shape my conduct and aspirations?"

What are your deepest values? Integrity, courage, health in mind and body, freedom, duty, service to others, frugality, philanthropy, discipline …

What are your most treasured pursuits? Intellectual endeavors, excitement, recognition, happiness, leisure, love, power, creativity, fun, passion …

The lists can be seemingly endless. Have you considered these questions before in moments of introspection? If so, what were your outcomes? Did you clarify your values on a piece of paper and carry it with you as you would a sacred map to immense treasure, or was the scrap of paper discarded in the busyness of the day? If you are considering these questions for the first time, don't rush the process. Allow your creativity to reveal as many examples of values and pursuits to your conscious mind as possible, and lock on to the ones that catch your attention and draw you close. It's important to know what you stand for.

Understanding and defining your value system is important because you must have clarity of choice in moments of decision. Should you accept that promotion? You've fought for it—you've yearned for the recognition, pride and income that it will bring—but ultimately your value system will determine if it is the right choice for you. Perhaps accepting the promotion will require stifling a value that is deeply important to you. You may be offered a bigger paycheck, but perhaps it comes with the cost of less freedom, less creativity or less time with your family.

Now your value system becomes a life-support system. If you don't know which value is more important, creativity or wealth or service or comfort, you will lack decisiveness in critical moments, and risk pushing away the greatest opportunities or accepting the worst ones for you. If you value adventure more than safety, or you value massive wealth more than comfort, you will make different decisions when faced with entrepreneurial opportunities. You must know what drives your soul, or you will forever frustrate yourself with a life created through inconsistent decision making.

3. Define Your Mission

Nothing happens unless first a dream.— Carl Sandburg

Passionate people have definiteness about them; they have a sense of mission, of overriding purpose. You can sum up the greatest men and women in just a few words that describe what their purpose was, what their contribution amounted to, where their focus pointed, where their passions lay. Say "Einstein" and we answer "relativity"; say "Edison" and we reply "light bulb"; say "Harriet Tubman" and we respond "Underground Railroad"; say "Henry Ford" and we answer "automobiles"; say "Donald Trump" and we offer "billionaire developer"; say "William Wallace of *Braveheart*" and we give you "Freedom for Scotland!"; say "Martin Luther King, Jr." and we say "non-violent reform."

What if we said your name? What few words would people use to describe you? Can you answer that yourself? Can you sum up your overriding mission in just a few words? What is it that you devote yourself to? Would you use words like *leader, achiever, innovator, general, entrepreneur, parent, artist, Olympian, orator, counselor, friend, warrior, visionary*?

Being able to answer this question cuts right to the essence of goal setting. What is the underlying foundation of purpose upon which you assemble your framework of goals? What is your ultimate mission? A home built upon quicksand will be washed away; a home built upon bedrock will be resolute. A life built upon whim and fancy will reflect that; a life built upon a clearly stated vision will reflect *that*.

You have been created with a unique talent; in all of history, there has never been anyone quite like you. You have a unique purpose to fulfill. There is something that you can do that is special, that you cannot delegate; you are the only one qualified for the task. There are things that you and only you can do, and this is what your life must be about. To distract yourself from following another path will not lead you to the highest summits that you seek. You will exponentially promote pleasure throughout your life experience by channeling energies into the passions that consume your mind and heart.

Your ultimate mission will likely be sewn together with the threads of your values, forming a patchwork of specific goals and action plans. Your values are the clue to your mission: What do you stand for? What would you die for? What would your risk your life for? What could you stand to lose, and what would dilute life of its meaning if it were to be stripped from you? What dream, once fulfilled, will leave you in a state of euphoria? What dream, if left unfulfilled, would crush you with regret? What do you want more than anything else in the world?

Take a moment and consider these questions. It is easy to shrink from this exercise. Henry Ford believed, " ... thinking is the hardest thing to do; that is why so few people do it." Consider the following examples of mission statements of different achievers, and use them to spur your own creativity:

- "I will be a living example of the excellence I expect from other people."
- "To be the best person I can be, consciously contributing positively to the world around me."
- "To build and lead our company in a way that shows integrity in action, respect for people and excellence in service."
- "To enjoy a life of great passion, adventure, and discovery, recognizing that there are no limits to my achievements and ultimate personal happiness!"
- "To reduce the violence in our beautiful cities by identifying and working to solve the underlying issues of poverty, crime, parental neglect and hopelessness in our disadvantaged youth."
- "I will serve my nation with bravery and honor, both on the battlefield and off, and help create a world that is safe for our children."

- "In my marriage, to enjoy our friendship together, to meet each other's love languages, to affirm each other's worth, to celebrate in times of victory, offer comfort through setbacks, and encouragement in the pursuit of our dreams!"
- "I will raise my children in such a way that they are contributing citizens, well-adjusted, self-affirming and encouraged to achieve in the areas of their greatest desires."
- "To share my creativity with the world."
- "I will inspire thousands of people to pursue and achieve success in every area of their lives, and empower them to inspire tens of thousands more."
- "To be a moral person in my deeds, a loving father to my kids, a devoted husband to my wife, a student of all humanity, a tireless servant of my faith and a fearless leader in my business."

Allow your mind to nurture these thoughts and rouse them from slumber if they have been dormant too long. A written statement of your mission will crystallize your values and desires into one core idea. Etch that idea into your mind. You know that there is magnificence waiting inside you to be revealed. What great quest will consume your days? What legacy will you leave to your children? Will these thoughts coalesce into an overriding, urgent drive that propels you forward? Will this signal one of the defining points of your life, where everything changed because you decided that now was your moment?

The time has come to stake your claim on the world in ways still greater than you have yet dared attempt. What are the words that will define the legacy of your days? Decide them now. Create them, capture them clearly and carry them with you forever. Let these words that define your mission become your battle cry through the days and years to come.

4. Reinforce Your Goals

Your goals must

- be exact
- be quantifiable
- be written
- have a written deadline for accomplishment
- inspire a burning desire
- be reviewed daily
- create focus
- be associated with believers
- be challengingly realistic
- be visualized as successful
- include a plan of action

How Do You Create Effective Goals?

As with any skill set, setting and achieving goals is a muscle that you will continue to strengthen throughout your life. You may have an intuitive sense as to how to achieve the thing that your mind is focused on; you may have resolved to become a student of this ability and immerse yourself in training materials previous to today. The basics will always remain the same, and masters in any field are highly proficient at the basics. True masters recognize that the most incremental increase in their proficiency with a fundamental skill will reap exponential rewards throughout their life. If you have accomplished much, but have struggled to accomplish a specific goal and have been wondering why, a self-diagnostic may be required. Have you violated or neglected any of the fundamental principles of goal attainment? Careful consideration of each principle may reveal a step you have deserted and reveal the key to breaking through the barrier to greater success you might be facing.

Define Your Goals

Clarity at the outset of your voyage as to your destination is paramount. Stumbling towards a vaguely defined outcome will diffuse your energies across different priorities, ensuring that you are emotionally and physically exhausted from your journey long before reaching port. What do you want? Precision in goal setting is the hallmark of excellence. Do you want to "improve" your health? Then get specific. Write down an exact goal; say instead "I want to increase my cardiovascular endurance by running 3km a day." Do you want to be "successful"? You must define success! Do you want to make "a lot" of money? You must name the amount! Say instead, "I will earn $200,000 this year."

Quantify Your Goals

How do you know when you've crossed the finish line? You must attach measurable criteria to your goals, so that you have a measuring stick to compare how far you've come from the starting point. In fact, being able to track your progress presupposes that you know what your starting point was! Using words like *more, better* or *greater* might be motivating, but they will ensure that you don't fully achieve what you could have if you had only been specific. Attach a precise measurement to your goal; put a numeric value next to it. If you want to "lose weight," write down instead, "I intend to lose 20 pounds." This way, you have an exact standard that you must attain in order to reach the goal! If you want to "save money," write down how much! $1000, $10,000, $100,000, a million? If you want to "expand" your business, describe what that means! Say instead, "I want a 20% increase in each order, and to increase our customer base by 10% in the next 90 days."

If it's a relationship that you want to "improve," name a specific behavior that you are committed to engaging and make your performance of that behavior something that you can measure. If you want to "improve" your marriage, decide what behavior would "improve" it … then measure the behavior! If complimenting your spouse is something that you don't do enough, set the goal of doing it three times a day minimum … and measure yourself! Skipping this step either leaves you vulnerable to washing out the results in the end, forcing you to be satisfied with meager progress, or leaves you frustrated with a perpetually moving target. Including this step ensures that you race past the competition.

Write Out Your Goals

The dullest pencil is more effective than the sharpest memory in recording our decisions, particularly when high emotion is involved. Taking pen to paper captures your integrity in the moment of decision. You see, your energies may fade. You may lose interest. You may face discouragement. You may play the mental game of dissuading yourself that you ever set the goal, that the goal at hand was ever important to you at all. But by putting the goal down on paper, you are now staking your integrity upon your assertions in moments of enthusiasm.

It's one thing to get excited and proclaim to the world that you'll do great and wonderful things; anyone can get excited in the moment of setting the goal. Leaders remain excited through the monotony of daily habit, of persisting through setbacks and bouncing back from disaster with their enthusiasm intact.

Write Out Your Deadline

Setting your target date for reaching your goal accomplishes several things. First, it assists in helping you work backward from your deadline to break the goal down into milestones for accomplishing your goal. Second, it spurs you into action once you realize clearly what must be accomplished *this moment* in order to reach the first milestone. Finally, it removes the "someday" syndrome that robs people of their dreams. Since "someday" will never come, by adding a deadline to your goal, you ensure your full engagement.

President John F. Kennedy boldly announced that Americans would land on the moon before the end of the sixties. When faced with this seemingly impossible goal, Dr. Wernher Von Braun realized by breaking the goal down into steps and working backwards, the first milestone was creating a viable rocket fuel. The deadline was the first year of effort. The deadline of one decade to land astronauts on the moon helped clarify the milestone of one year to create the rocket fuel, and within the first year Dr. Von Braun had accomplished his first goal. The rest is history. Without the greater deadline, he would not have launched into such fervent action and achieved the success that he did.

Have a Burning Desire to Accomplish Your Goals
Passion will not be deterred by obstacles, but a weak interest will. One man with a burning desire will outperform 100 men with a strong interest. A burning desire attracts like-minded partners to your quest; you will become a magnet for opportunity. Your unerring enthusiasm will convert people to your cause and reveal greater opportunities. A burning desire will carry you through the night when you are physically exhausted. It will compel you to take action and dare greatly, where lesser men and women will hesitate, leaving you free to claim your prize. Your desire will force your creativity to discover answers when disaster strikes and all hope seems lost. As the adage says, "There are no hopeless situations—only men who have grown hopeless about them."

Review Your Goals Daily
In life, you get exactly what you focus your energies on. Daily review of your goal keeps it at the forefront of your mind,

channeling your energies towards your most important initiatives. The common man or woman directs their energies towards fending off the daily assault of minutia, crisis and distraction. The uncommon man or woman has a razor-sharp vision of their purpose beyond the whirlwind of the moment; such people are building their future, not just simply surviving through the emergency of the day. Disaster will get your attention all by itself; the future of your dreams will not. Just as we must pay our investment account *first* in order to achieve our greatest financial destiny, so too must we pay our dreams *first* if we are to achieve our greatest personal destiny.

What you think about most, you will literally become. Whatever goal you focus on the most consistently, you will manifest. Daily focus on your greatest dreams is one of the most powerful weapons in your arsenal, and one of the first tools to be left by the wayside by self-proclaimed "experts" on goal setting. Do you carry your written goals with you at all times? Are they on your person at this moment? Did you look at your #1 goal today? You know your answer.

Stay Focused

When he arrived in the New World, Cortez gave the order to burn his ships. As his soldiers stood in stunned silence, watching the ships reduced to ash, Cortez reminded them that they were not here to *try* to win—they had arrived to *conquer*. Since the possibility of retreat had been removed, the soldiers faced one of two outcomes: win the battle, or face certain death at the hands of their enemies. With no option to withdraw, the soldiers were well motivated to prevail, and they conquered their foes with great determination. Their only focus was victory, and they achieved it.

Diffusion of focus is the antithesis of great achievement. It is difficult to dabble in a multitude of interests and expect to achieve excellence in any of them. Does this preclude you from having a variety of interests that you should permit yourself to enjoy? Of course not; it simply means that if you merely tinker with something, it's not realistic to expect momentous results when you are offering a distracted, half-committed effort. Hobbies will not earn you the greatest rewards in life. The rewards come only from those endeavors that consume your time, energy and focus.

Reading your goals each day is the first step to focus. The next step is having the goal consume your every waking thought, your every decision, your words and actions. People should not be able to have a 30-minute conversation with you without having your passionate focus come up in discussion at least once. Motivational psychiatrist Dr. Steve Stokl asks, "What is that single molecule on the tip of your white-hot spear?" You only have so much time, so much energy within you, and while your reserves of energy may be great, the ability to direct your powers onto one singular point of interest will dramatically expand the impact of your efforts.

Associate with Believers
The slightest chink in your armor may be all that is required to render you open to attack. Since your mind is your greatest tool and your confidence your greatest alley, ensure that their protection is inviolate. If you currently associate with negative naysayers, and they continuously berate you and disparage your innermost dreams and goals, you have two choices. First, you may wisely choose to be more selective with whom you share your goals. If people you associate with are not supportive, you cannot afford to allow their pessimism to seep into your mind and poison your determination. Be selective with whom you trust sharing your greatest aspirations, for dreams are tenuous

and can be wounded relatively easily when they are still little more than a thought in your mind. You need every advantage, logistical as well as psychological, to dare greatly and succeed.

The second option, if you face naysayers, is to simply disassociate from them; if someone is attacking your goal, you may elect to remove that person from your circle. This may be a family member or friend, and you may choose to warn them in advance of this drastic measure, explaining that they are threatening your relationship by continuing their negative behavior.

Recognize that a naysayer may also be a well-intentioned loved one who cares about you dearly. In this instance, he may not have the same belief as you, or have the same access to the information that you have. As well, the loved one may have different values and goals than you have; he may be negative because the attainment of one of your goals means the failure of one of their own goals. Be alert to this and take your observations into consideration.

Make Your Goals Challengingly Realistic

If your goal is impossible, you won't even step up to bat to attempt its acquisition. If it is possible, though, ask yourself if the goal is too small to fire your enthusiasm. Too small a goal might leave you disinterested; too great a goal might leave you feeling discouraged at the starting gate. Most goals are possible—even if you are not yet sure how to attain them. Never allow a lack of obvious resources, skills, experience or significant examples of success to deter your enthusiasm and belief in yourself! Motivational speaker Les Brown says, "If any one has done it … then it is possible that I can do it!" You must be pressed to engage your talents and feel that the reward is worth the effort, and you must at some level believe that you can accomplish what you desire.

Is it realistic to expect that you will reach your goal? That depends upon several factors. What are your available resources? How much time, money and physical energy do you have available to devote to the achievement of the goal you have selected? Based upon your current schedule, available resources, action plan and your effort, is it reasonable to expect that you will accomplish your goal? Sometimes, we will set goals that are completely unreasonable, usually because we don't have the resources, our action plan is not viable, or we are not following the plan we have designed. You must ask yourself, "Based upon my current skills and abilities, if I expend the effort I am willing and capable of offering, is it realistic to expect that I will meet my desired deadline?" If not, then you must either increase your effort, improve your abilities or change your deadline.

Please note that I have not said *realistic goals* but rather, *challengingly realistic goals*. If the only goals ever set were mired solely in realism, we would not have automobiles, space travel, common software on every desktop, or a map of the human genetic code. Every great endeavor would have collapsed under the immense weight of it being *"unrealistic"* at the time of its inception. Realism, when orphaned from challenge, is simply pessimism under the false guise of wisdom. The soldiers that gave their lives on the beaches of Normandy so that we may enjoy freedom today did not do so using realism as their code of honor. They used valor, courage, determination and the belief that victory was challengingly possible.

Visualize Success

You will manifest success first in your subconscious before you enjoy the tangible rewards of success. You will believe it before you see it. Fully engage the power of your subconscious mind to harness your ultimate abilities. Engage all of your senses; create the image of your achievement so clearly in your mind that your subconscious literally believes that you have already accomplished what you have set out to do. See yourself doing the great thing. Hear the sounds of the applause. Feel the textures, smells, colors, tastes, the emotions you will experience in the moment of victory. Play the movie of your success over and over in your own mind, stimulating all of your senses.

Ultimate champions will go a step further, and dictate the affirmation of their ultimate victory onto tape or CD and play it repeatedly over and over to themselves. Eventually the details of their success will become so entrenched in their mind that the experience takes on the sensation of a euphoric memory. If your mind thinks that you've already achieved victory, you will attract your success so much more rapidly than any effort previously attempted, that you will never leave this step out of your goal-achievement process again.

5. Develop Your Action Plan

- Break down your goal into milestones.
- Monitor your progress.
- What resources will you require?
- Create a buffer for emergencies.
- Are there any conflicting goals?
- Prepare for obstacles.

You don't need an action plan to initially imagine the goal or believe greatly in your ability to accomplish it, but you will need it in order to find your greatest success. You would not attempt to erect a skyscraper without a detailed plan of action, nor should you expect that you will fulfill your mission without a clear agenda and strategy to achieve your goals. Successful goal setting includes clearly documenting the major and minor steps that you will traverse along the journey to your goal.

Do not mistake this for meaning that you must know every detail of your journey before you start; in fact, the opposite is true. Many people suffer from "paralysis of analysis" and are frozen with fear because they do not know exactly what will happen in all circumstances. You can rest assured that despite your best laid plans, some obstacle that you did not anticipate with reveal itself along your journey. Expect surprises. There is a clear line between foolhardy and ill-equipped voyages into the unknown, and a keen sense of adventure that says "we'll figure out the rest as we go." Binoculars were invented to reveal the path before the adventurer. Mentors, analysts and action plans are required to reveal the path before the entrepreneur. Boldly take the calculated risk; there comes a point in each quest when you must resign yourself to facing the unknown ahead and say, "I have prepared as well as possible; the journey must begin."

Your action plan is the final step in preparing for the life you want. You have clarified your goals, shaped the words that define your mission, selected goals that align with your highest purpose, and now you can document the strategic movements that will bring you success.

Break Your Goals Down into Milestones

By defining the date for accomplishing your goal, and the measurable quantity attached to your goal, you can begin to chart what must be accomplished each day, week, month and year that leads up to your ultimate deadline. It is human nature to procrastinate. Setting and honoring milestone goals prevents the frenzied rush of last-minute effort that plagues procrastinators.

If you have six weeks to complete a task, break the task down into six milestones. That way, if you have fallen behind on your production one week, that Sunday night you must breathlessly force yourself through the discomfort of meeting the weekly target. Facing the small discomfort of honoring milestones prevents you from facing the massive discomfort of doing a rushed, shoddy job in the end (or worse, enduring the heart-wrenching pain of missing your goal entirely). If you want to lose 20 pounds in 10 weeks, then a reasonable weekly milestone would be 2 pounds a week. If you want to save $12,000 this year, then each month your milestone goal is $1000. If you are currently taking your executive MBA, develop a study schedule for your upcoming exam that is realistic.

Monitor Your Progress

The master goal achiever knows exactly where they are on the path to success at each moment; the well-intentioned runner-up does not. Setting milestones prevents running out of time in the end, but you must consistently check to see that you are reaching them. Setting a milestone and then forgetting about it is fruitless; setting a milestone and remaining aware as to how much time remains before each deadline is powerful. Do you have to be a clock-watcher to succeed? Absolutely not. But if you miss your first milestone, clockwatching may be a skill you should consider if that was the reason for the miss. If you're checking your progress once a month and you are falling behind, consider checking it once a week. Increase your concentration until you get on track and stay on track.

What Resources Will You Require?

An effective action plan takes into account all of the necessary tools to complete your task. Three major resources are obvious:

- **Relationships** Who will you need to work with? Whose experience will you need to draw on? Whose connections will you require? Whose permission will you need to acquire? From which organizations will you require participation? What will you require from your family and friends, either in active or passive support? Do you have people cheering for your success?
- **Skills** What will you need to learn? What experience will you need to gain? What do you need to be able to do? What training will you require to prepare for your final attack on the summit? What do you not yet know, and what is your plan for acquiring this knowledge?
- **Material Resources** What capital is required? How much time is needed? How many people do you need to hire? What materials do you need to acquire? Do you have the physical energy to complete the task? Do you have the available time in your schedule, taking into account your other priorities and goals? If not, have you made plans to free up your time by re-evaluating your goals and changing deadlines for less important tasks?

Once you have identified the required resources, you must develop plans to acquire them. Can your ultimate plan begin on schedule with some of these resources missing? What is the most critical and urgent resource required that will halt the initiation of your action plan? If something is required, your entire schedule of deadlines and milestones is at the mercy of acquiring this pertinent resource. You must build preparation time in at the beginning of your action plan to allow yourself to assemble the tools required to reach your goal.

Create a Buffer for Emergencies

If you need to close $1,000,000 this year in new residential real estate sales above your quota, and three months into the year you are falling behind on meeting that target, you don't want to leave it till December 29th to start playing catch-up. Life does not allow many opportunities to play catch-up, so you need to plan in advance for potential setbacks. You already know that something will throw you off track. Rather than being surprised and getting caught unprepared, plan in a buffer for completing your goals in advance. You may decide to set your personal deadline for 10 percent earlier than the ultimate deadline; if emergencies occur, you still have a 10 percent buffer of time to complete the task at hand. It is unrealistic to expect that things will always flow smoothly and that you won't face setbacks; you know well enough that this is not the way of the world. However, it is tempting to push yourself harder than you already are, to convince yourself that no buffer is necessary and that everything will come together exactly as planned without oversight, error or delay. Learn from previous experiences you've faced dealing with unexpected emergencies, and resolve to always build buffer time into your best-laid plans.

Do You Have Conflicting Goals?

One goal is fine; 20 may be too many. When you are designing your action plan, are you taking all of your other ongoing projects and goals into account? How much time and energy do the other goals require, and will they impede your progress with the goal you are currently considering? Will taking action on one goal mean that you must drop the pursuit of another and, if so, which one is truly the priority? Which one yields the greatest return on investment?

As well, it is entirely possible to pursue more than one goal at a time, but not if they contradict deeply held values. Perhaps you have resolved to go dramatically out of balance for a period of time in order to launch a business and move your entrepreneurial dreams forward. You are free and justified in doing so if getting the reward is valuable to you. However, what if you have just received a physical from your family physician, and she has warned you that your blood pressure is dangerously high and you must engage in daily cardiovascular exercise? Will your work goal contradict your health goal?

What if you have set the goal to add more significance to your life and engage in volunteering at a local shelter or as a Big Brother or Big Sister, but you also have the goal of spending more time with your own son or daughter? What if you are motivated by the pursuit of adventure for one goal and motivated by the pursuit of comfort for another? Conflicting values will diminish your effectiveness. It is absolutely possible to set and achieve multiple goals, as long as your execution of each action plan does not contradict another goal.

Be Prepared for Obstacles

You know they are coming. You have already built extra time in your schedule to handle them, but what will you face around the corner? It is not possible to anticipate every type of challenge or potential setback, but it is possible to brainstorm the potential realities that you may face. What could go wrong? Is there someone who has gone through a similar process and achieved a similar goal? If so, can you reach out and discuss with them the challenges that they have faced? A mentor will perceive obstacles before you do.

Brainstorm the problems you think you might face. Running out of money? Time? Having trouble reaching your customer base? Managing your emotions, staying calm and focused? Not being able to nurture the relationships that you need to?

Not being able to learn the appropriate skills in time? Being unprepared? Marketing challenges? Facing enemies that wish you the worst? Dealing with the response of your competition? Gaining the support of your family and friends? Combating your own fears? Managing daily discipline?

What is your contingency plan for potential setbacks? You may not want to dwell on the negative, believing that high achievers focus solely on the positive and that a great attitude will carry you through any emergency. More accurately, a positive attitude will overcome a feeling of defeat, when and if you face setbacks, and spur you to creative thought and taking action to overcome the odds. A negative attitude will succumb to setbacks. A positive attitude does not protect you from life; it merely arms you for life.

If planning for a rainy day is not your strength and is something you find to be mentally and emotionally distracting, you must ensure that you delegate this task to a trusted advisor. Pessimists play a useful role in working alongside visionaries, because they will spot the potential problems that the eternal optimist will gloss over—until it's too late! Don't internalize negativity; merely consider the validity of that point of view. Could there be a weakness in your plan that proper preparation might address? The ultimate analyst to have by your side will see the weaknesses, but have a positive and preventative mindset so that you can be prepared in advance and ready to defeat obstacles should they arise.

Summary

A goal is an objective, a purpose. A goal is more than a dream; it's a dream being acted upon. A goal is more than a hazy "Oh, I wish I could." A goal is a clear, "This is what I'm working toward."
—David. J. Schwartz, *The Magic of Thinking Big*

The key to spreading passion into each nook and cranny of your daily experience is to clarify what fires your spirit. What do you want from your life? Is there something calling to your spirit that you have long ignored, the faintest whisper of dissatisfaction that you could be doing more with the time you have? Have you tried to quiet this voice because you felt that your dreams and goals were impractical, that "realistic" people wouldn't fancy pursuing the adventures that stir your soul? Is there something magnificent inside you that you want to share with the world, something that would leave you breathless with happiness if you would only take action on it? Can you do, have and become more than you are today?

At all times, leaders know that there is always more. More that they can do to strengthen their character. More that they can do to nurture the love in their family. More that they can do to expand their empire. More that they can do to share their creative genius. More that they can do to shape their body and fill themselves with health and vitality. More that they can do to reach and serve more and more lives. More that they can do to build a monument that will outlive their mortal existence. More that they can do to feel a greater sense self-esteem and happiness, enjoying a life-long romance with themselves. The race for excellence knows no finish line.

And so, a life of passion begins with a blueprint to achieve your passion. It begins with deciding how the finale will look. The first and most fundamental of skills required of you is that you know exactly what you want.

Action Steps
1. Visualize the End Result
Take a moment and imagine your own funeral; what would you like the people from the various areas of your life to say about you?

2. Clarify Your Values
What is truly the most important value to you? Integrity? Adventure? Achievement? Health? Love? Jot down all of your values and organize them in order of importance to you.

3. Define Your Mission
Write out a first draft of your mission statement. You will likely refine these words and ideas over the next few weeks and months as you change and grow as a person. Start with one to three sentences, using your eulogy statements and values as guideposts to inspire you.

4. Select Your Goals
Brainstorm without limitations. Don't cloud your mind with concern over details, logistics or viability. Dream without limits. What are all of the goals that you want to set, in each area of your life? Set short-term (90 days), mid-term (one year) and long-term goals for the areas that inspire you: your mind, body, spirit, career, finances and relationships. Feel free to use the checklist below as inspiration in order to spur your creativity. And remember: once you've set your goals, follow each principle of success we've discussed to ensure their success!

Examples of Possible Goals
Mind
❐ Maintain a positive attitude
❐ Expect the best in all situations

❏ Sharpen my memory by 10%
❏ Learn to speak Spanish
❏ Learn a new skill
❏ Identify a fear and take action
❏ Listen to motivational CDs
❏ Read a self-improvement book each month
❏ Increase confidence by speaking up in key meetings
❏ Be aware of my personality's "rough edges" and decrease them by __%

Body
❏ Lose 20 pounds
❏ Cardio-vascular endurance: Run 3 miles a day
❏ Complete a 26-mile marathon
❏ Eliminate junk food from my daily diet
❏ Eat six small meals a day
❏ Work out intensely for 30 min, 2 times a week
❏ Hire a personal trainer 3 times a week
❏ Eat daily multivitamins
❏ Reduce daily caffeine intake

Spirit
❏ Review my values and mission statement in solitude
❏ Spend a weekend this month in nature to enjoy inner peace
❏ Volunteer for a cause I believe in
❏ Enjoy a creative pursuit
❏ Learn to play a musical instrument
❏ Invest 20 minutes a day reading Scripture
❏ Nourish my faith

Career
❏ Invest in training to increase my value
❏ Develop a plan for my next promotion

❒ Call on 20% more customers a week
❒ Volunteer to lead the committee
❒ Launch a new business venture
❒ Raise $1 million in venture capital
❒ Improve customer service by…
❒ Follow up sales with thank you notes
❒ Brainstorm marketing ideas to increase market share by __%
❒ Attend night school to get my Executive MBA

Finance
❒ Save 10% of my income
❒ Take a course on investing in stocks
❒ Purchase a house for rental income
❒ Increase income by 20% this year
❒ Read books on money management
❒ Create a wealth mastermind team
❒ Create 3 strategies: mere survival, material comfort and wealth
accumulation

Relationships
❒ Attend my son's football games this season
❒ Write letters to friends & family
❒ Enjoy a vacation
❒ Commit to being home for dinner at 6 pm each night
❒ Set aside a weekly "Date Night" with my spouse
❒ Spend quality time with my kids
❒ Connect with my best friend
❒ Have that difficult conversation with a family member
❒ Love my spouse in the way he or she wants: tell, show, touch
him or her.

2 emotional mastery

> If you are distressed by anything external,
> the pain is not due to the thing itself but to
> your own estimate of it; and this you have
> the power to revoke at any moment.
> —Marcus Aurelius

We are convinced that men or women who can master their emotions are without equal. No door can be crafted that can refuse them entry. No disappointment can scar their spirit or mar the purity of their vision. The obstacles before them will wither under the sunlight of their confidence, their assurance, their unyielding calm and inner peace, and the strength of will that they command. Those who can master their emotions, who can conquer their own mind, can accomplish any goal that they set for themselves. They will lead families, they will lead corporations, and they will lead cities and nations. ***The person who can master their emotions is able to do the single most difficult act imaginable: they are capable of leading themselves.***

To have a passion for life means that you engage life with utmost enthusiasm and vigor. It means that you use your positive energies and emotions as a tool in order to achieve your dreams. It does *not* mean that you wait to achieve your dreams, and *then* become passionate. The measure of a person's character is what they do, where they are, with what they have. The ability to control your emotions is one of the most powerful skills in the world. Think of the men and woman who have shaped our world. Political leaders like Winston Churchill, Abraham Lincoln, Benjamin Franklin. Think of scientists and inventors like Thomas Edison, Isaac Newton, the Wright Brothers, Albert Einstein. Think of entertainers like Steven Spielberg and The Beatles. Think of philanthropists and social activists like Albert Schweitzer, Mother Theresa, and Ghandi. Think of technology pioneers and giants like Bill Gates and Steve Jobs. Every single one of these men and women share one common trait: at the pivotal moments of their lives, when the great drama of their story was unfolding before them, they each shaped their world by controlling their emotions.

Goal setting is the blueprint for building your dreams. Emotional mastery is the strength to pick up the hammer and get the work done. All achievement, all monuments to the human spirit, can be traced back to an intractable channeling of massive positive thought. This creates a shield against negative thoughts and pessimism. Shielding our minds against doubt and poisonous self-talk is as vital as defending our mortal bodies from the ravages of cancer. Optimistic thought is the fulcrum against which all massive achievement is leveraged. To have reign over our emotional lives is to have reign over the course of our destiny.

Perception versus Reality

How we see the world is based on our beliefs. Often experience teaches us we need to change these beliefs.

What Shapes Our Perception?

We are the lens through which we see the world. Steven Covey says, "We see the world, not as it is, but as we are." We may look at the same photograph and see different things. We may listen to a conversation and hear different things. One person may see the glass is half empty, while the other person sees that it is half full. We may have an argument, and despite having both been involved, we might walk away and firmly believe that different things were said! Perception is merely our subjective experience of objective reality.

Your psychological lens is shaped by your beliefs, previous experiences and emotional state at the moment. If your camera lens has a scratch on it, every photograph you take will include that scratch. In time, you may simply begin to think that the entire world has a scratch on it. A person's lens may be scratched by racism, prejudice, abuse, or failed dreams, or it might be polished to a shine with positive role models, experiences of compassion and grace, and memories of bravery. In the movie *The Abyss*, a female engineer speaks about the paranoid soldier, Coffee. She says, "Coffee sees Russians; he sees hate and fear. You have to look with better eyes!" In a sense we are all like Coffee; we need to realize that we are filtering all of our experience of the world through our own eyes, ears and mind.

If we wear rose-tinted glasses, the world will appear rose-colored. If we believe that people are generally good, we will notice the good deeds that they do. If we believe that people are generally shifty and crooked, we will look for examples when their character has fallen short, and we will no doubt find those examples. If we were raised to believe "money doesn't grow on trees," we might see scarcity and hoard our pennies in fear. If we were raised to believe "money is created through hard work and ingenuity," we might see financial opportunity and abundance.

If we are religious and have positive role models, we may believe that all humans are equal in the eyes of their maker and seek mutual respect in our dealings. If we have been taught to hate another religion and to strike back violently against a group of people, we may feel justified in doing so.

If we see the negative in things, we will believe that disaster is the normal state for people, and we will perceive the glass as half empty. If we see the positive in things, we will see the glass as half full. If we see possibility in things, we will see the glass is filled completely with water and air!

We Have the Freedom to Choose Our Attitude

Dr Viktor Frankl was a German psychiatrist trapped in a Nazi concentration camp during World War II. The horrors that he was forced to face and endure are unimaginable. He watched his family brutally murdered in front of him. He was beaten and tortured. He was deprived of food, comfort and dignity. In time, he became desensitized to the death and suffering around him. He was only spared from the gas chambers because he had been given the "privilege" of unloading the dead bodies; after all, someone needed to be left alive to clean up the mess.

In the midst of this horror, he was struck with a vision of his wife; a memory of her smiling, of a loving moment they shared. He basked in this memory and felt great warmth, happiness and love lift his spirits. He realized that by simply thinking of a happy memory, he had created the emotional experience of happiness in himself. In the midst of all of this suffering, torture and death, he was stunned to discover that he could still experience happiness. The prisoners could tell jokes to one another, make each other smile, laugh out loud, and the crushing weight of sadness could be lifted for a moment.

He began to see that certain prisoners were more adept at surviving than others. They were healthier; they lasted longer.

What set them apart? Dr Frankl identified a common trait: the prisoners that survived longer had a more positive attitude. They would go from person to person, sharing their last piece of bread, consoling their friends, whispering, "Somehow, we'll make it. Someday, we'll be set free. Someone will rescue us."

In his monumental work, *Man's Search for Meaning*, Dr Frankl shared his epiphany. He realized that the Nazi guards could beat the prisoners. They could take away their food. They could make them get up at a certain time or go to bed at a certain time. They could humiliate them, degrade them, torture them and even murder them, but the one thing they couldn't do was make them feel a certain way about it. In fact, the last thing that could be taken away from the prisoners was the ability to choose their emotions. He said, "The last of the human freedoms is to choose our *attitude* under any given set of circumstances." People can do things to us and say things to us; catastrophe may rain down upon us and the ground open beneath our feet. Every day, bad things happen to good people. But with every circumstance, we still get to choose how we think and feel about it. We get to choose the meaning that we attach to these events. After everything outside of us is lost, we still get to choose our internal attitude. The question then becomes: what attitude will you choose?

Focus on the Positive

Whether you think you can or think you can't, you're right.
—Henry Ford

What is it about human nature? Once we are secure, we become complacent. Once we have food, we never think of what it is like to be hungry. Once we have stable income, the worry lifts and we may take it for granted. Once a nation achieves political freedom, some people become apathetic about voting. The blessings that are obvious to those less fortunate are quickly forgotten when the blessing has become commonplace to us.

But take that freedom away, and we will fight with our every fiber to regain it. We don't consider the plentiful supply of oxygen we have until we are trapped underwater or develop a respiratory disease. We don't consider the strength and mobility provided by our legs, until we are faced with a wheelchair. We are slow to see the good side of a loved one, until they are lost to us. We don't treasure the irreplaceable hours and minutes that our mortal bodies are left with, until the ticking hand of the clock approaches our own personal midnight. We ignore all of the gifts that we enjoy and squander our focus on what is missing. We trade thankfulness for displeasure.

If you are to make your life a masterpiece, you must decide from this point on that your mind is your most powerful tool and directing its positive energies is your most important task. You must make the decision to see the good over the bad. To see the opportunity over the challenge. To see the possibility over the setback. To see the strengths over the weaknesses. You must learn to direct your mind to focus on the positive over the negative.

Of course, you know people whose lives are based on the opposite principle: they focus on what's wrong with a situation, instead of what's right. These people defend their position by saying, "We're being realistic!" Just scratch a realist and you'll find a pessimist hiding beneath the thin veneer. Realism demands that you objectively evaluate the situation at hand. Perhaps you wake up to discover, "We've lost our biggest customer! Fifty percent of our business has evaporated in one day!" This is the reality of your plight, and you should acknowledge this.

But a pessimist will add to that, "We've lost our biggest customer—and we're doomed!" A possibility thinker will observe the situation and say, "We've lost our biggest customer—and now we are free to replace them with someone even bigger!" A pessimist says, "We don't have time to turn it around; our bills are looming large, we have a payroll to meet … we may as well not even try!" A champion says, "We've been in tough spots before; this is the time for action. We have the skills, experience, energy and confidence to attract success and make it through the day!"

A positive mental attitude is an intellectual decision to look at the best possible side of things. It demands that you have the faith that the best possible outcome is attainable and within reach. Both optimist and pessimist use the powerful tool of imagination and attach their own meaning to events as they unfold. They ask, "What does this mean?" when they are faced with a challenge, and they imagine the result. A pessimist says, "It means disaster" and an optimist says, "It means opportunity." When David faced Goliath, the other men retreated as they cried, "He's so big, we can't defeat him!" David looked at Goliath and thought, "He's so big, I can't miss!"

Being positive does not involve ignoring reality, it means creating the image of a positive outcome in your mind. Faith means that you use your imagination to create a bright future, and fear involves using your imagination to create the darkest storm clouds on the horizon. Why is there such a disparity in how people look at things? Why does one person see that they are destined for success, and another person assumes that defeat is his or her fate?

It depends upon what thoughts you allow into your mind.

What Is Your Mental Diet?

If you owned a Formula 1 race car, you would chastise your pit crew for putting a low-quality fuel into the engine. If you owned a million-dollar thoroughbred race horse, you would endeavor to provide the highest quality feed. If you were coaching an Olympic gymnast with the goal of claiming the gold medal, you would put her on the strictest of diets with the highest nutritional value for her body.

Yet we indulge in foods that provide no nutritional value and are harmful to our health. We recognize the obvious wisdom in not indulging in bad foods and blithely gloss over one of the most important diets that determine our fate: our mental diet.

What do you allow into your mind on a daily or even hourly basis? What instructions are you feeding into the billion-dollar computer that resides in the six inches between your ears? At all times, the internal recording device is capturing and archiving every sensation, every sound and sight and smell, our entire experience of the world through our senses—and our mind is also recording the emotional meaning we attach to these sensations.

Olympians show merciless discipline when it comes to accepting only the best food into their bodies, and leaders show merciless discipline when it comes to accepting only the best thoughts into their minds. Life is never static. At every moment, we move a step closer to ultimate success, or slip backwards. The computing acronym GIGO, which stands for "Garbage In, Garbage Out," applies to your mental diet as well. Every idea that slips past the gatekeeper at the door of our mind is programming our belief systems, augmenting our confidence or diminishing it, altering our view of the world for the better or for the worse.

Success in the tangible world begins first with success in your mind. Napoleon Hill says, "Whatever the mind of man can conceive and believe, he can achieve." If your mind is dwelling on the greatest qualities of human kind, on the highest ideals of human excellence, on success story after success story, on all of the reasons that you have the capacity and skill for greatness, then your mind will direct your actions with unbridled power towards the object of success. "The strangest secret in the world," says Earl Nightingale, a pioneer of motivational speaking, "is that you will get exactly what you think of." If you dream for, plan for and prepare for success; if you act with confidence and seize opportunities, believing all the while that success is assured, then you will be successful. If all of your thoughts and energies have but one positive aim, then the story of your life's course will land clearly on the mark, just as the arrow will fly from the archer's hand to the target.

However, if the archer misses the target, who or what should he blame? The arrow? Or the people around him? Or his parents for not training him properly? Should the archer blame the world for not making the target easier to hit? No! The credit for precision and the fault for inaccuracy belong directly to the person wielding the bow. The archer points the arrow, draws tight the string, and sends it where he directs it.

So you must ask yourself: where are you pointing your thoughts? Toward your ultimate goal? Toward what you want your life to be? Are you thankful for all the blessings you enjoy? Or are you pointing your thoughts towards the pessimistic reasons why you believe you won't make it? The great Wayne Gretzky didn't focus on the opposing players on the ice. He focused on the open spaces between them and used his vision to make plays.

The world will provide a constant stream of negativity to indulge your senses. It is almost impossible to escape its presence. So, understand how your mind works: you cannot choose to think about nothing. You cannot remove a negative thought with zero thought. You must substitute a negative thought for a positive one. If you are watching a scary and violent television show, the second best way to rid your mind of its effects is to turn it off. The best way to cleanse your mind is to change the channel. If you turn on the nightly news, you will be greeted with the disasters of the day: what building burned, what plane crashed, what CEO was arrested, whose car has crashed, which hero has fallen, whose life has been destroyed. Decide to turn the channel. It's certainly important to know what's going on in the world, but what benefit is there in allowing your thoughts to wallow in the depth of human misery and suffering? Make your mind a fortress against negativity. Make your thoughts strong and pure and heroic. Make yourself focus on what can happen, what could work, what you are capable of. Direct your mind to seek answers, instead of seeing only the problems.

What steps can you take to ensure the most powerful and positively influential thoughts retain the position of superiority and dominance in our mind? Here are the most powerful strategies.

Read Biographies of Excellence
Our history is filled with examples of men and women to whom we can aspire, who showed great courage, compassion, initiative and grace. Reading their biographies allows us into their minds, to converse with them and be mentored by them, even though we may be separated by centuries. Allow the greatest human beings who have ever lived to come alive in your life, and apply their direction to your actions. What lessons can you learn from Abraham Lincoln? From Nelson Mandela? From Anne Frank? From Benjamin Franklin? From Lance Armstrong? From Rudy Giuliani? From Mahatma Ghandi? From Helen Keller? From Winston Churchill? Let their stories whisper in your ear when you must make challenging decisions; let their words of courage help draw up your strength when you face insurmountable odds. Let their positive beliefs galvanize your own.

Associate with Winners

A candle loses nothing in lighting other candles. If you spend time with winners, their flame will serve to ignite the best within you. But, the opposite is also true. Hang around negative people, and their pessimism may douse your flames. Parents are reluctant to allow their children to hang around with kids who are a negative influence. The reason? We begin to act and think like the people we spend time with. It is nearly impossible to avoid being influenced by a thought process or ideology to which we are consistently exposed. Our only recourse is to associate with people who are going places and be very selective about whom we allow to influence us. Just as we improve our tennis game by playing with an "A" player, so too do we improve our mental game by associating with a winner. Steel sharpens steel, and conversely a rotten apple spoils the bunch. Heroes beget apprentices who in turn blossom into heroes in their footsteps.

Cherish Your Memories of Victory

Don't dwell on your mistakes; dwell on your moments of genius. Don't look through the photo album of setbacks that you save up in your mind; train your sight to review the moments where you pressed on against terrible odds and emerged victorious. Look at what you've done right, at your gifts and talents, at the moments when your character was true and your intent was just. Create a monument in your own mind of all the good that you have done, and see your moments of valor, see the flashes of brilliance, see the deeds of compassion, see all of the best that is within you.

Are you being egotistical? Not unless you are imagining these events. You are practicing selective memory in the face of monumental negativity. It is our nature to see the worst in ourselves, and the world around will be quick to remind us of where we have failed before. There is no hero who hasn't faced defeat. But the strongest among us can draw on the images of success in that critical moment. There are a few moments which shape our entire lives, and when your moment comes, you will act based upon the image you hold of yourself. Anyone who has ever won is a winner. Do you see yourself as a winner? You are a winner, and you should see yourself as one.

Listen to Positive Messages

Time spent driving between home and work is often unproductive. Champions squeeze every last bit of usefulness out of the underutilized moments they discover through the day. Don't just sit through traffic; let the greatest minds of our time and the times before us speak to you. Seek out and purchase audio books that feature the speakers who have systems of thought that you want to reinforce or adopt as your own.

Let their words of success whisper to you throughout the unproductive moments of your day.

Read Uplifting Words

Our libraries and book stores are filled with the wisdom of the ages. Read the most powerful books on success-oriented thinking that you can find. Develop a voracious appetite for understanding the minds of men and women who are the people you wish to emulate. Choose to focus on positive writings just before you go to bed, and just as you wake up in the morning; the last 10 minutes before we drift off to sleep are those moments when our subconscious mind is the most open to programming. Choose to program your mind with the best thoughts. Decipher the secrets of the greatest minds that have walked before you. Let their ideas shape yours. Let their beliefs challenge yours. Remember that if you think differently from someone, and they have a great success in an area that you desire to excel in, then you should consider

changing your beliefs and internal dialogue to more closely reflect that of the champions you admire. Create an environment of
positive thought. Surround yourself with positive statements and
affirmations that are uplifting and motivating to you.

Speak Positive Words

Words have power. Our subconscious has absolutely no sense
of humor. Whatever you say to yourself with great intensity
and emotion will become deeply ingrained in your innermost
thoughts. How you conduct yourself verbally is a mirror to your
self-image and view of the world. Do the words you share re-
sound with confidence, possibility and excellence? Or do your
words drip with weakness and defeat? Choose the vocabulary
and speech of champions. Choose to frame things in the most
positive light, seeing the possibilities that exist beyond the reality
of the challenges you face. Recognize that there are no problems,
only challenges. A failure is a learning opportunity. A disaster
is an opportunity for character development. Frustrations are
an opportunity to practice patience and forgiveness. Become a
master communicator by using words of power and possibility.

Dress for Success

Let the world know that you are coming to claim your prize. A
positive mind is housed in a positive body, which is presented to
the world through your choice of dress. Do you look like a winner? Do you carry yourself like someone going places? People sum
each other up visually in the first few seconds of meeting. When
people meet you, does your appearance say, "I am going places?"
You don't need to wear an Italian silk suit to make this statement
to the world, but a grease-stained T-shirt may not be the best bill-
board for the greatness within you. When you look in the mirror,
are you dressed like the person you want to become?

Every field and endeavor is different. Dressing for success will require very different styles when one person's success is leading an investment team on Wall Street, and another person's success is getting a million-dollar record deal for their punk rock band. Ensure that you think, speak, act and look like the person you want to project.

Cleanse Your Mind of Negativity

Chase out pessimistic thoughts. If you catch yourself dwelling on a problem for a greater time than the solution, let the alarm bells go off in your mind that your focus is not on success. Are you harsh and critical in your mind? Do you secretly sneer at people and wish them the worst? Do you offer vile criticisms in the quiet recesses of your thoughts? Or are you just as loving in your mind as you are to the world? We must oust any poison in our system, whether it is chemical or mental. And the poison may not just be directed at others; we may be putting ourselves down too. Even in the private sanctuary of your most personal thoughts, the battle for success is won or lost on how you talk to yourself. How do you speak to yourself? Do you celebrate your wins, or admonish yourself for the smallest error? Most people are harder on themselves than they are on any other people. The negative talk that many people inflict upon themselves is literally abusive. If we had a friend who spoke to us the way we might speak to ourselves, we'd drop that friend like a hot potato. Become your most cherished and beloved friend. Become your greatest cheerleader.

Ask Better Questions

Some men see things as they are, and say, "Why?" I dream of things that never were, and say, "Why not?"
—George Bernard Shaw

Our mind is like a camera. Where you point your camera will determine your outlook on life. If you want to improve your attitude, you can begin by simply pointing your camera at what is right about a situation, rather than what is wrong.

Consider the following illustration. What do you see in the space below?

•

Most people would respond by saying, "I see a dot." However, others would respond by saying, "I see a whole lot of perfectly pristine white space, with a barely noticeable dot in the middle." Ninety-nine percent of the above space is untouched, and 1 percent of the above space has a blemish. Focus on the 99 percent. The exceptional mind will see what is positive in a situation, rather than what is wrong. Winners will focus their energies on a positive solution, rather than complaining about the inconvenience and discomfort that the problem poses for them. A winner says, "How can we fix this?" A loser laments, "I don't see a solution, so why bother trying?"

When you catch yourself complaining, ask yourself, "Am I focusing on the dot?" Are you looking at the 1 percent that is wrong with a situation or the 99 percent that is right? People wake up in the morning and grumble that they *have* to go to work. Winners wake up and realize they *get* to go to work. Look to see the reaction of the unemployed person who is about to lose her house if she bounces another mortgage payment. Wouldn't she be bursting with gratitude to have the job you have?

People complain that their house isn't big enough, yet how quickly they would long for it if, if they had escaped from their native country into a nation of freedom with only the shirts on their back and were forced to move into a one-bedroom apartment with 10 other people for the next six months. People complain that their children irritate them, are noisy and messy and cause such headaches, but how many parents endure the heartbreak of miscarriage after miscarriage, dreaming of having a child that would make a mess in their home? People complain that their spouse gets on their nerves, that they bicker and complain, yet how quickly would they dream of holding their spouse even for a moment longer if their spouse were serving in the military and killed in battle? Over and over, we see that many people forget how incredibly lucky they are and take the greatest blessings of their life for granted, choosing instead to gripe about the small inconveniences they face each day.

We have so much to be grateful for. Do you pause each day and consider how lucky you are? What are the blessings in your life? Food in the refrigerator? A warm bed? Do you have a source of income? A car? A computer? Do you have friends and family who love you? A phone to call them with? Are you lucky to live in a free nation where you can vote, travel, speak, think and worship as you please? Lucky to have a mind that functions with normal capacity? Can you run, laugh at a joke, taste chocolate, listen to symphonies, enjoy a sunset, smell your favorite foods, feel the warmth and softness of your loved-one's skin against yours? Are you lucky to be free of disease? Do you feel lucky to be alive? If you answered *yes* to most of the above, you are wealthy beyond the dreams of most human beings alive on the planet today. You must choose to see your wealth.

The next time you are faced with a problem, ask yourself, "Why am I so lucky that I get to solve this problem? Why am I so fortunate that this challenge has been given to me to solve?" When you ask better questions, you get better answers. Your subconscious will seek out the answers to whatever question you pose. You may ask yourself a question, and hours later the answer may pop into our mind out of nowhere. If you ask, "What's wrong with this situation?" your brain will supply you with answers. If you ask, "What's wrong with my job, my paycheck, my house, my kids, my spouse, my life?" you will come up with defeatist answers. If you ask yourself, "What is fantastic about my job, my paycheck, my house, my kids, my spouse, my life?" you will come up with possibility answers.

Courage Conquers Fear

Cowards die many times before their deaths; the valiant never taste death but once.
—William Shakespeare, *Julius Caesar*

Todd Beamer did not know that courage was required of him on September 11, 2001, when he stepped onto his doomed airplane. Shortly into the flight, terrorists seized the plane and murdered the crew, taking control of the cockpit. Soon, the passengers learned through whispered conversations on their cellphones that the twin towers in New York had been struck by planes commanded by other suicidal terrorists. The passengers of that ill-fated flight quickly realized that they were condemned to die that day. The plane had been taken off course and was now over Pennsylvania, likely headed for the White House. The passengers knew what was required of them. Todd phoned his wife to say that he loved her, that his fate was sealed, but they still had a chance to save many other innocent people on the ground from dying. With the rallying cry of "Let's roll!" Todd Beamer led a group of passengers and stormed the cockpit. In the most courageous act possible for a human being, they forced the plane into the farmer's fields of Pennsylvania, sacrificing their lives in order that others would be spared.

What makes a man a hero? Where is the wellspring of courage that surfaces within his soul in the critical moment? We know that many people rise up as they are called upon in challenging situations, but for every story of courage under fire, there are a thousand untold stories of men and women who have remained true to their values in daily life, who gave their all when everything counted.

Do we need to see combat to rise up and show courage? Absolutely not. Opportunities for displaying courage arise every day. We can show courage when we are offered a bribe to cover up information of illegal activity, and we turn down the money. We can show courage when we see a woman with a bruised and battered face, and we confront her husband about spousal abuse. We can show courage when we feel tempted to have an illicit affair at a business convention, and choose to say no. We can show courage when a friend is getting into her car drunk, and we force the issue and take away her keys. We can show courage when we are battling cancer. We can show courage when we are proposing to our spouse. We can show courage raising venture capital, writing a book, starting a family or pursuing any dream in our hearts.

But many people die with their dreams still in their body, and fear has nailed the coffin shut on their dreams forever. What dreams lie within your heart that have yet to see the light of day? Is fear the major barrier to you achieving the success you desire? Is it stopping you from having a passion for life? Do you worry that you plan won't work, that your idea lacks merit, that you can't rally the troops, that you won't be able to raise the funds, that you can't mend the relationship, that you aren't experienced enough, aren't capable enough, aren't deserving enough?

When we are born, we only have two natural fears: the fear of loud noises and the fear of falling. Every other fear is learned. Being afraid to seek a romantic relationship is a learned fear. Being afraid to speak in front of a large audience is a learned fear. Being afraid of facing rejection during a sales presentation is a learned fear. The Mongols who assaulted the Great Wall of China did not have to break the wall down; they merely bribed the guards to open the gates. Similarly, breaking through your barrier of courage merely requires that fear gets past your mental gates. Fear just needs to make a convincing argument as to why you will be defeated—and you have to believe the lies that fear is whispering to you.

And so, many men and women retreat from the source of their fear. They avoid defeat. But conceding to fear is defeat! Helen Keller says, "Life is either a daring, bold adventure, or nothing." What will your life be if you tremble before every adversary? What will become of you if you lose the race because you never entered it, if comfort is the only decision-making factor in setting your goals? It isn't comfortable to push through fear. But your very life hangs in the balance! If you give in to fear, if you allow it to control your fate, what becomes of you? What will the final report card on your life read? Will you feel proud of yourself or profoundly saddened? Mark Twain challenged us not to be ruled by our fears in this quotation. "Twenty years from now you will be more disappointed by the things that you didn't do than by the ones you did do. So throw off the bowlines. Sail away from the safe harbor. Catch the trade winds in your sails. Explore. Dream. Discover."

People with courage do not lack fear. Many times, people with courage do experience fear. But courage is not the absence of fear; it is the presence of brave action in the face of fear. The great spoils of battle go to the man or woman who embraces fear and pushes through his or her discomfort to victory. Terrence said, "Fortune favors the brave." The courageous among us will ignore the feelings of past setbacks and the whispers of past defeats, and refuse to believe that their past equals their future.

What have you been putting off in your life because of fear? What bold adventure has fear dissuaded you from embarking on? What dream has yet to see the light of day because fear is winning the case in the courtroom of your mind? What tremendous joy and happiness would you bring into your life if you could have, do and be everything you've dreamed of? How long will you allow yourself to be constrained by the fear you have just imagined? When will you resolve to face your fear and push through it?

When you do the thing you are afraid of, something miraculous happens. You realize that the thing that you feared isn't so big after all. You look behind the curtain and realize that the Wizard of Oz is simply a frightened, tiny man. You feel a surge of power and confidence sweep through you when you realize that you no longer have to be confined to the fear that you have harbored. Action conquers fear. You can take inspiration from Ralph Waldo Emerson who wrote, "Do the thing you fear, and the death of fear is certain."

Adversity Builds Character

Every adversity carries with it the seed of an equal or greater opportunity.
—Napoleon Hill

As a teenager, Michael Jordan failed to make the tryouts for the high school basketball team. His competitive spirit forced him to confront his coach, and they agreed to meet through the summer and practice for the next few months. Michael pushed past his initial setbacks and became the greatest basketball player that has ever lived. Abraham Lincoln, one of the most revered U.S. Presidents of all time, was a dismal political failure for most of his life, facing numerous defeats throughout his entire career.

Tiger Woods is the most celebrated golfer competing today, and is quickly catching up to the records set by Jack Nicklaus. But Tiger is black, competing in a predominantly white sport, and has faced racism during his rise to fame. In 1952, Sir Edmund Hillary attempted to climb Mount Everest, the highest peak on the planet. He reached 29,000 feet up, but he failed to reach the summit. In his anger, he screamed at the mountain, "You have beaten me, but you are not going to grow any more ... and I will continue to grow!" He returned the next year and conquered Everest, becoming the first man in history to do so.

Beethoven had become completely deaf by the age of 46, yet went on through his loss to create some of his most inspired works. Oprah Winfrey was fired from her broadcasting job at the age of 22. Silken Laumann was struck by another boat just 10 months before the Olympic rowing event she was favored to win, and her lower leg was shattered. But through searing pain and heartbreaking effort, she rehabilitated herself in record time and claimed the bronze medal.

What are the stories of adversity you have faced? You may not be able to control the things you go through. In fact, sometimes things happen for no good reason at all. They just happen. Life is just going to kick you sometimes. The difference between people who overcome or get crushed is in how much they decide to allow the hurt of the adversity to define their existence. Do you choose to use adversity as a tool for greatness? Do you allow the adversity to make you stronger? Do you search for lessons within the adversity and use them to become wiser? All great monuments of achievement carry with them the battle scars of adversity in their construction. You will face adversity. How you face it will determine your outcome. Mike Murdock succinctly expresses this attitude when he says, "All men fall. The great ones rise again."

Stand on the Shoulders of Giants

One of the most powerful ways to bolster our own courage is to look back upon the courageous acts of great men and women who have come before us. We realize that if they endured such terrible odds and overcame them, perhaps we too can be as steadfast and brave in our actions. As we read the biographies of great leaders, the words that their minds have chosen and captured can serve to inspire and lift our own spirits. Seek out the writings of men and women that you regard as heroic, and use their words to inspire you.

President John F. Kennedy

There is no strife, no prejudice, no national conflict in outer space as yet. Its hazards are hostile to us all. Its conquest deserves the best of all mankind, and its opportunity for peaceful cooperation may never come again. But why, some say, the moon? Why choose this as our goal? And they may well ask why climb the highest mountain? Why, 35 years ago, fly the Atlantic? Why does Rice play Texas?

We choose to go to the moon. We choose to go to the moon in this decade and do the other things, not because they are easy, but because they are hard, because that goal will serve to organize and measure the best of our energies and skills, because that challenge is one that we are willing to accept, one we are unwilling to postpone, and one which we intend to win, and the others, too.

Source: **Speech delivered in 1962 at Rice University, Houston, Texas**

Theodore Roosevelt

It is not the critic who counts; not the man who points out how the strong man stumbled, or where the doer of deeds could have done better. The credit belongs to the man who is actually in the arena; whose face is marred by dust and sweat and blood; who strives valiantly; who errs and comes short again and again. Who knows the great enthusiasms, the great devotions, and spends himself in a worthy cause. Who at the best knows in the end the triumph of high achievement; and who at the worst, if he fails, at least fails while daring greatly. So that his place shall never be with those cold and timid souls who know neither victory nor defeat.

Source: **The Man in the Arena**

Dr. Martin Luther King, Jr.

Well, I don't know what will happen now. We've got some difficult days ahead. But it doesn't matter with me now. Because I've been to the mountaintop. And I don't mind. Like anybody, I would like to live a long life. Longevity has its place. But I'm not concerned about that now. I just want to do God's will. And He's allowed me to go up to the mountain. And I've looked over. And I've seen the Promised Land. I may not get there with you. But I want you to know tonight, that we, as a people, will get to the promised land. And I'm happy, tonight. I'm not worried about anything. I'm not fearing any man. Mine eyes have seen the glory of the coming of the Lord.

Source: **Sermon delivered in Memphis, Tennessee on April 3, 1968, the day before he was assassinated.**

Winston Churchill

You ask, what is our policy? I say it is to wage war by land, sea, and air. War with all our might and with all the strength God has given us, and to wage war against a monstrous tyranny never surpassed in the dark and lamentable catalogue of human crime. That is our policy.

You ask, what is our aim? I can answer in one word. It is victory. Victory at all cost—Victory in spite of all terrors. Victory, however long and hard the road may be, for without victory there is no survival.

… I take up my task in buoyancy and hope. I feel sure that our cause will not be suffered to fail among men. I feel entitled at this juncture, at this time, to claim the aid of all and to say, "Come then, let us go forward together with our united strength."

Source: **Speech delivered to the people of Britain, May 13, 1940.**

You can learn and become all that you need to be. Fear has the insidious side effect of clouding our minds to the strengths that we possess. But courage and daring have the opposite effect. Courage makes our minds sharp, toughens our emotional skin, mobilizes armies, and can defeat your foes without firing a single round. Faced with a protagonist brimming with unstoppable confidence, many of your enemies will lose their will to fight simply because they know that you've already won the battle in your own mind. They see that you have stepped into the ring to merely let the events leading to your victory unfold, just as your courageous mind has predicted they would.

Motivation Defeats Procrastination

If something is inconvenient, uncomfortable, or anxiety-provoking, yet it is morally, legally and ethically the right thing to do... you MUST do it! Otherwise, your self esteem will plummet.
—Dr. Steve Stokl

Sometimes we feel that we have to move mountains. How do successful people overcome the feeling that some challenges are just meant to be put off for another day?

Rewards versus Consequences

Some people may feel that lacking motivation is the primary cause for the struggle that they face in achieving success. If you have ever felt unmotivated, you can rest assured that it is not because of an inherent lack of ability on your part to take action. There is no character flaw that forever labels someone as "unmotivated." Everyone is highly motivated—under the right circumstances.

In fact, there are always two conditions that can guarantee a high degree of motivation:

1. You face an inconceivably massive reward for doing something (either because you really enjoy doing it, or the result itself is intoxicating);
OR
2. You face imminent disaster if you don't immediately take action.

There are two forces that direct human behavior. Anthony Robbins sums this up by saying, "Everything you and I do, we do either out of our need to avoid *pain* or our desire to gain pleasure."

Consider any moment in your life when you have felt unmotivated, and left a task until the last moment. During the entire process, you knew that you had a deadline. But in each moment of our lives, we are faced with options and the necessity to decide upon those options. Our decision-making process involves asking ourselves at some level: "What will give me more pleasure? Doing the work in front of me, or going out and having fun?"

Most people will jump at the opportunity to enjoy immediate pleasure, and put off the discomfort of work for another time. The seductive nature of a fun-filled activity can lure us away from something unpleasant, particularly if we are self-directed and are not immediately accountable to getting the task done. Giving in to immediate gratification is the blueprint for short-term satisfaction. But being motivated by delayed gratification is the blueprint for long-term victory.

An excellent example of this is exercise. You do not need to exercise today. Barring the most extreme medical cases, it is highly unlikely that any harm will come to you in the next 24 hours if you don't hop on the treadmill or get to the gym this evening. But what about five years from now?   10 years? How about 20 years? The impact of your decisions builds as life moves on. And the person staring at you in the mirror 20 years from now is a reflection of those decisions, whether it is in the tightness and tone of your muscles or the unattractive flab, in the grooves worn into your face from years of laughing in celebration or from scowling with disdain.

And so the mental games begin. When faced with walking on the treadmill for 20 minutes this evening, you may ask yourself, "What would be more pleasurable: working out, or taking it easy?" You may choose resting on the couch and enjoying a television program. Every human being uses this decision-making process every day, in every situation. And what you consider pleasurable will determine your ultimate fate.

What would you find more pleasurable:

- Finishing a report, or going dancing?
- Putting money into retirement savings, or buying a new plasma-screen television set?
- Hitting the "snooze" button and staying in bed, or keeping your job?
- Avoiding the difficult discussion with your spouse, or facing the conflict and working towards resolution?
- Being honest on your tax return, or "cooking the numbers"?
- Staying late at work or being home for your daughter's birthday party?
- Buying a new car now with high-interest loan payments, or driving the modest car that your long-term financial strategy suggests?
- Eating a candy bar or eating a salad?
- Taking a risk, or risking nothing?

Your fate is shaped by your decisions. Your decisions are guided by your application of the principles of pain and pleasure. The key to motivating yourself in every situation is to recognize that you already know how to get motivated: when the reward is very high, or the consequences are immediate and drastic. In order to conquer human nature, we need to either increase the immediate reward we receive from doing a task, or create an artificial deadline with uncomfortable consequences, and force ourselves into action.

Listing the Pros and Cons

When motivating yourself, choose to employ the carrot before using the stick. Make it fun and desirable to take action on your task. Benjamin Franklin would employ a "T" bar where he listed the pros and cons of a situation. You may choose to ask yourself, "What is everything positive that I will achieve and enjoy when I accomplish this task? What are all the positive feelings I will enjoy? These might include pride in a job well done and heightened self-esteem. What are all the material rewards I will reap? What are all the good reasons why I should do this task?"

Now consider the negative. "What will happen if I don't do this task? How will it make me feel? What will I lose or not gain? What will it take away from my life in the coming days, months and years if I do not make progress in this area? What will be missing from my life?"

Consider all of these thoughts in detail. The more compelling argument you can make for taking action, the more rewards you can list on the pro side and the more negative consequences you can stack on the con side of your list, the more engaged in the task you will be. Add the additional factor of high emotion: do you really care about these rewards and consequences? Are they meaningful to you? If not, you will either need to drop the goal, or intensify the reasons for taking action. Sometimes we can motivate ourselves simply by thinking about the reasons we've listed in this exercise. Highly proactive and accomplished people get things done because to do so is in line with their character. They say, "I am responsible, and a responsible person gets the job done. To violate my character is too painful to imagine; far more painful than taking action. I derive pleasure from acting in a way that is consistent with my self-image. Doing so will feed my self-esteem."

Increasing the Rewards

Sometimes, the internal motivation is not enough to spur us to action. Realize that it is our nature to act when the reward is significantly bigger than the effort. If simply thinking about the benefits is not motivating, you have to up the ante.

Create a new reward that you can enjoy immediately upon completion of the task and that is commensurate with the amount of time, energy and resources involved in the work. If you have to do a small task, design a small reward. If, in your mind, you have to move the Earth, then the size of the reward must skyrocket in value. Perhaps it is as simple as a small treat; you resolve to buckle down for the next 20 minutes on the task you've procrastinated on, and you'll earn a break and a nice snack. Until then, no break and no snack. Many times this simple game can spur you to action. Perhaps you resolve that you will get to watch your favorite TV program for having finished the report ahead of schedule, or go to your favorite restaurant for having completed spring cleaning in your home.

In order for this to work, you have to feel that getting the reward is more stimulating than avoiding the work. If the first reward you select doesn't light your fire and the effort still eludes you, increase the reward until it overshadows the work. Make the reward so grand that you are delirious with excitement to achieve it, so that the effort of the work becomes insignificant. It may involve attaching a greater personal meaning to the result. It may require some creative thought as to how to make the process of work more fun and exciting. It may involve promising yourself a material reward or an exciting new "toy" to tempt you into action. It may involve connecting the work with helping other people. The more personal and emotionally charged the reward, the more inspiring it will be.

Increasing the Consequences

The great challenge to motivation that you will quickly realize is that people may be somewhat tempted by the carrot, but will leap into action to avoid the stick. People will expend more effort trying to avoid receiving punishment than they will invest in vying for great treasures. Pain is a greater motivator than pleasure. If you have gone through the process of intellectualizing a pros-and-cons list, seconded with the effort to motivate yourself with rewards, and you are still unmoved, it is time to apply a little negative pressure. You must turn up the heat.

Start small with consequences. No need to become a masochist in order to be highly motivated! Begin with denying yourself simple pleasures. Resolve that your smallest pleasurable activities and treats are set aside until the task is accomplished. You cannot partake in the fun activity you'd love to indulge in until the work is done. You can't have that favorite food. You can't make that exciting purchase.

If you find you have still not taken action, the next steps are obvious: continue escalating the consequences until they become unbearably uncomfortable, and the task you are avoiding looks like a vacation compared to the self-inflicted punishment you are enduring. Canadian entrepreneur Kevin Kooger says, "Winners are willing to do today what others won't, so that they can do tomorrow what others can't." What are the buttons that you can push to motivate yourself? Perhaps the idea of having to endure cold showers each morning until you take action will compel you to act. Perhaps you were looking forward to a fun weekend, but you resolve that you must finish your work first in order to go. Perhaps you were going to purchase a home theatre, and you resolve that you haven't earned it until the work at hand is done. We all have our own buttons; the key is to identify what is unbearably uncomfortable for you.

Do you want to quit smoking but feel insincerely motivated? Just link unbearable consequences to your actions. Imagine how it would feel to look your children in the eye and tell them how much you love them. Tell them that you want to live long enough to see them finish university, get married and hold your grandchildren in your arms. Tell them that you promise to get medical help and quit because you love them and that every day they can ask you if you've kept your promise to quit. And then imagine telling them that any day henceforth that they see you with a cigarette, it means that you don't love them, and that you're secretly hoping that you never get to experience any of those happy moments. Which is the greater motivator for you: your behavioral need for the cigarette between your fingers? The social need to chit-chat with your buddies outside the office? The physical yearning for the nicotine in your bloodstream? Or is the greatest motivator the desire to prove to your kids that you love them? You decide.

Strategies to Overcome Procrastination

Here are some creative strategies to help you kick the procrastination habit.

Resolve to Get Started

Inertia is your enemy. Once you get the ball rolling, it's amazing how much you can accomplish. When the space shuttle launches into the atmosphere, the majority of its rocket fuel is expended just lifting itself the first 12 inches off the launching pad. Overcoming inertia is a monumental task. Keep in mind that the "journey of 1000 miles begins with a single step." Don't consider if you have the energy to finish the race. Don't consider if you have the energy to keep up with the competition. Concentrate your mind on simply getting off the starting blocks with determination.

Take Initial Action—Block Off a Small Unit of Time
Decide that you are going to dedicate 10 minutes to getting something accomplished on your task. You don't feel that you have the time to finish the task? Then block out 10 minutes to start the task. If a task is going to require hours of effort, the thought of all the time involved may be too overwhelming to contemplate. Break the task into manageable, bite-sized pieces. Instead of thinking, "I have 10 hours of work ahead of me," and feeling paralyzed with that realization, choose instead to say, "I am going to sit down at my desk and accomplish 10 minutes of work."

Take a Ridiculously Small Action
Instead of thinking, "I've got to get dressed in my gym clothes so that I can go to the gym and work out for one hour," choose instead to simply get into your gym clothes. Don't plan on exercising. Stand there, dressed in your shirt and sweat pants, running shoes on, water bottle in hand—and don't go to the gym. After a few moments, you may feel silly not going to the gym, since you're already dressed! If you are avoiding a sales call, don't make the call. Just sit at your desk. Next step: pick up the phone and place it to your ear. Don't call; just hold the phone. Sit there holding the phone for 20 minutes and just try not to make a phone call.

Remind Yourself of the Pros and Cons
Ask, "What bad things will happen if I do this? What great things will happen? How great will I feel about myself when I do this?" What are your rewards and punishments? Keep them in the forefront of your mind. Fill your thoughts will how delicious victory will taste when you claim it. When you catch your energy waning and your focus drifting off target, simply indulge in imagining the unbearable consequences you have assigned if you miss your deadline.

Leverage Your Self-Esteem and Self-Worth

Tell yourself, somebody at my level wouldn't wait to act! You are too important. You are too credentialed, too accomplished to add this disappointing performance to your resume. Your life is too valuable to squander on mindless distractions and empty pursuits. You have too much greatness to share with the world, and only a lifetime of years allotted to you. No time can be spared. The value of an hour of your life is immeasurable.

Never Allow Fatigue, Disappointment or Fear to Dissuade You

Lesser men and women make decisions based upon whether they feel like doing the work. Winners make decisions based upon whether they feel like earning the prize. Second-place is given to those who play the movies of their past defeats in their minds; the spoils of battle go to those who play the memories of success over and over in their minds instead. Your weaker emotions will tempt you to capitulate and give up. Fear may grip your heart and whisper stories of defeat into your ear. Your warm and cozy bed will beckon. But this is not your true nature. It is in your nature to win, to press on, to brace your spirits against loss and continue into the night while others rest. Let them wake from their slumber and wonder how once again you have succeeded them in the race. Let them cry foul, claim favoritism and argue that luck shined upon you—and they may claim all of this while you wipe the weariness from your eyes and the sweat from you brow on the winner's side of the finish line.

Summary

In the times when my load seems too great to bear, I'll draw strength from my sense of duty. In the times when I must endure defeat, I will do so with dignity and honor. Where others falter, I press on. While others cower, I prevail. When failure breaks the spirits of other men, it serves merely to strengthen my resolve. I am the embodiment of persistence! It is when no one else is willing to do it, when people say it can't be done, that is the greatest time for victory!—CJ Calvert

Winners make the decision to master their emotions. They choose to look at the good in a situation and ask, "What is great about this?" They choose to fight past fear and claim victory. They choose to launch into action and overcome the great weight of inertia that binds other men and women to a lesser existence. When combined with positive thought, courageous action and a heightened state of motivation, the description of your swift movement towards destiny will be summed up simply. What one word defines the progress of champions?

Unstoppable.

This single word can be your calling card, your introduction of yourself to the world, your self-branded signature of excellence in all encounters. It is your answer to negativity, to fear, to procrastination. It implies that you are on a mission, that your mission is of value, that it is fraught with obstacles that could dissuade lesser people, and that you are not one of them. This single word can be the exclamation point of your life. *Unstoppable* says that you have consciously decided that your brief sliver of existence will stand for something, that there is greatness within you and that the message you seek to share with the world was first ingrained within your own heart. It can be found within the mastery of your emotions and the activities you engage in daily. It can be shared with those you have the pleasure to meet and greet in your daily adventures. You can show positive thought, courageous action and great motivation with every move you make. You can enjoy a life of passion. You can master your emotions and become—unstoppable!

Action Steps

1. See the Positive in Situations

Examine your outlook on life over the coming days. Do you gripe and grumble behind the wheel? Do you smile and say hello to people? Are you forgiving of people and assume they had the best of intentions when they wrong you? It is easy to feel that we are positive; it's time to do a self-diagnostic and confirm that belief. Over the next week, consider your mental state and outlook on life through your daily experience and rate yourself on a scale of 1 to 10, with 10 being the most optimistic and positive person imaginable.

2. Improve Your Mental Diet.

What are you feeding your mind? Monitor your mental diet and consider whether you turn on the news more quickly than you turn on an inspirational CD. Make a point to increase your positive input on a daily basis, either through reading or listening to positive message CDs. Minimize your association with negative people. You may choose to institute a five-minute rule: if a good friend or family member is a chronic complainer, you agree that after five minutes of negativity (or less!) you walk away from the conversation.

3. Take Courageous Action in Spite of Fear

What has fear kept you from doing in your life? Robert Schuller asks, "What would you do, if you knew you couldn't fail?" Take a moment and brainstorm what you would do if the possibilities were limitless, if success was assured. Give your imagination the gift of courage. Would you have a different career? Pursue different hobbies? Improve your relationships? Shape your body? Build investments? Create a new business? Go after your dreams? It is time to build your courage muscles. Select one thing that you have been holding off on doing because of fear and resolve to take action.

4. Break Through Procrastination

Have you been avoiding taking action on other priorities because of reasons other than fear? What have you procrastinated on? Identify three tasks that you have fallen behind on (or perhaps not even started) and write down what the deadline is for their accomplishment. Next, select a reward that you will enjoy when you accomplish each. Select a consequence that you will face if you do not meet the deadline. Choose three people to speak with about your new commitment and promise them that you will take action and complete the task on time.

3 relationship mastery

In everyone's life, at some time, our inner fire goes out. It is then burst into flame by an encounter with another human being. We should all be thankful for those people who rekindle the inner spirit.
—Albert Schweitzer

Exceptional relationships can serve to fan the flames of your passion, helping to bring your dreams to life. In times of discouragement, they can lift you up. They can bring their passion to the table and combine it with yours, creating new and powerful ideas, products and services that never would have seen the light of day if you had not combined forces. When you are struggling creatively, relationships may offer a small idea or suggestion that lights the fireworks of new possibilities in your mind. They can take the baton from you hand and return it back to you, allowing your efforts together to create massive synergy. They can take your *good* idea and make it *great*.

The oft-quoted story of the conception of Post-it® notes describes Dr. Spence Silver, a scientist at 3M who was trying to develop a new adhesive. The experiment failed, because the adhesive he created was weaker than originally intended. History credits Dr. Silver as the original inventor. While this is true, it was actually his colleague, Art Fry, who served as the catalyst for bringing the good doctor's idea to market. Art Fry would go to church and feel frustrated that he kept losing his page in the hymn book. While looking for a bookmark for his hymn book, Art remembered the story of his friend's adhesive. It took 18 months to get the product to market, but they finally did. The world would have never seen Post-it® notes without the relationship of those two men.

The point is this: as talented as you may be, it is not possible to do it all by yourself. There is no human being who has achieved greatness without the assistance of others at some level. Whether it is a mentor showing you the ropes, your business partner being a sounding board for ideas, your spouse encouraging you during the rough times, or your secretary simply taking your phone messages, absolutely no one gets there alone.

> Goals are the blueprint for your success.
> Emotional mastery is the strength to pick up the hammer.
> But *relationship mastery* determines your ability to lead the team of workers who will help you build your dreams.

As an individual, you may master goal setting and managing your emotions. But are you going to hammer every nail? Who is going to steady the ladder or hold the other end of the two-by-four? Behind every massively successful person walks a dedicated army of relationships. Without other people, you will need 100 lifetimes to complete your life's work. You only have 24 hours available each day. You will multiply your effectiveness by learning to live and work well with others.

As well, building a mansion may not be considered a sign of success if you are sitting by yourself in the new house, feeling lonely. Passionate relationships make it all worthwhile, both personally and professionally. Humans are social by nature. Relationships are a key component to being successful because we, as a species, are social beings. Success built independent of others will not be as fulfilling when enjoyed in solitude. Any success that we are able to share with other people can feel more fulfilling than the successes that we have no one to share with. If we make it to the top, but we've lost our loved ones along the way, what have we really achieved? Is it important to you when you finally reach that pinnacle you've been yearning to attain that you have someone you love beside you to clink your champagne glass with and offer you a heartfelt congratulations?

Lying in your hospital bed, in the twilight of your life, will your material possessions be beside you, to comfort you? *No.* What about your bank statement, showing the financial wealth you have amassed? What about the awards, the trophies and the medals you have won? All of these things are worthwhile things to achieve, but they are a by-product of a life lived well. Material possessions are simply the contrails that are written against the blue sky of your life, proving that you were fast enough to break the sonic barrier of success in the jet aircraft of your career. No, the greatest bank account of wealth will be the collection of people's names that you include in your personal ledger: how many people you would describe as being dear to you, and how great your love for them is. Count your fortune in terms of the quality and number of relationships you enjoy and you will have found incredible personal wealth.

Leaders Master the Art of Building Relationships

Leaders are different in a very specific way from winners; although we have referred to both winners and leaders throughout this book, being one does not necessarily guarantee that you are also the other. A winner is someone who crosses the finish line. A winning leader is someone who crosses the finish line with others, and waves the checkered flag for the people coming in behind them. Therefore, being a leader presupposes that that you are leading people. And the art of leading people successfully presupposes that you have mastered the skills of building and maintaining effective relationships.

Does having a prestigious job title on your business card make you a leader? No. Positional leadership simply means that someone reports to someone else, as defined by the organizational chart at your company. It doesn't guarantee that the positional leader is effective, enhances morale, clearly communicates objectives, has a high-performing team, or even has the respect of his or her team. Being a positional leader means, at best, a good performance from your staff that reflects well on you, and at worst, an unproductive performance because your staff sabotages your efforts.

Effective leadership does not require a title. Gandhi had no official designation, no formal powers, yet he was able to influence the people of India so magnificently that he toppled British rule in India forever.

Does owning a company and being a multi-millionaire make you a leader? Perhaps in part. How about being the best at what you do and being hailed as the leader in your industry? Maybe. How about being a living example of the excellence you expect from others? Possibly. While all of these things may be part of the makeup of a leader, they are still missing one key ingredient: your effect on other people. When Lawrence of Arabia set out across the desert by himself to attack his Turkish enemies from the land, he was not yet a leader. At that moment, he was simply a heroic and determined man. However, once his brave example inspired hundreds of other men to follow him across the desert and fight by his side, then he became a leader of men.

Can you stir people to action through cruelty? Through manipulation? Through fear? Only temporarily, if at all. You can be sure that you are not getting their best effort, and that they will be plotting their escape—and likely hoping for your downfall, as well. Leaders understand how to engage, capture the interest of and mobilize people by using positive strategies.

Leaders have the ability to create, foster, and maintain long-lasting and fulfilling relationships with other people, both personally and professionally. In its simplest form, a leader is someone who makes you want to listen, join their cause and take action. Only those who commit themselves to mastering the principles of effective communication, who commit themselves to understanding the personalities and motivations of the significant people in their life, and who see the inherent value in others can achieve the greatest success through leadership. Mastering the art of building and maintaining effective relationships will maximize your ability to achieve your dreams.

Create an Effective Relationship Blueprint

Keep away from people who try to belittle your ambitions. Small people always do that, but the really great make you feel that you, too, can become great.—Mark Twain

What will it take to build effective relationships? Two things: being a quality person and inviting quality people into your life. It's a two-way street. So what makes a quality person, and how will you recognize them in a relationship with you? Quality people always have a positive influence on your life. You will always see that your life is better because they are part of it. They stand beside you to celebrate your great victories, and console you during times of loss. High quality relationships are far different from fair weather relationships: they stick through the good times and the bad.

How do you decide who to allow into your life? How do you determine who qualifies for your time? This will depend upon your definition of a great relationship. What are your standards? To what standard do you hold the people around you? Do you uphold the same standards that you expect of others? Do you expect people to be uplifting, flexible and considerate of your feelings, but do not feel that you need to offer those qualities in return?

Think again. If you treat people badly, expect the good ones to drift, if not run, away. And if people treat you badly, they should expect (and you should show them) that you won't tolerate anything but the highest standards in relationships. Enforcing those standards depends first upon knowing what they are.

What is your blueprint for an effective relationship? If you could describe the qualities of a great relationship, what would they be? Consider the following examples, and see if you would want a friend or partner who has these qualities:

- ❑ Is positive and respectful
- ❑ Is rejuvenating and re-energizing
- ❑ Picks you up when you are down
- ❑ Encourages you to pursue your dreams
- ❑ Helps you see the best qualities in yourself
- ❑ Catches you doing things right
- ❑ Holds you to a higher standard of excellence
- ❑ Makes others' needs a priority
- ❑ Believes in you
- ❑ Makes you know without qualification that you are a better person because of the relationship.

The best relationships bring positive blessings into your life. When Henry Ford was trying to build his company, he faced a serious challenge in the earliest days: he had designed his revolutionary engine, but did not have the money to build a prototype. One night, he was tossing and turning night in bed, trying desperately to figure out how to raise the $600 for the blacksmith to create the prototype of his engine block. Suddenly, his wife sat up in bed and suggested that they could cash in their life insurance to get the $600. She supported him. She believed in him. His success would be their success; her focus was to help him discover a solution.

Positive relationships add value to your life. The best people will encourage you during challenging moments, and your success is a priority to them.

Who's Packing Your Parachute?

Is it possible that we may take people for granted, that we may overlook the incredible blessing that they bring to our lives? Absolutely. You may have the great fortune of having someone in your life right now who emulates all of the qualities of a positive relationship, and you offer him or her nothing in return. Is that person your spouse? Friend? Colleague? Employee? Are you quick to overlook the small considerations that people extend to you and slow to offer thanks or even return their favors? If so, this could be one of the greatest relationship barriers in your life.

As you think more about the blueprint for an effective relationship, make the decision to open your eyes to the wonderful qualities of the people around you. It is entirely possible that you are overlooking some of the most special people right under your nose.

Charles Plumb was a U.S. Navy jet pilot in Vietnam. After 75 combat missions, his plane was destroyed by a surface-to-air missile. Plumb ejected and parachuted into enemy hands. He was captured and spent six years in a Vietnamese prison. He survived the ordeal and now lectures on lessons learned from that experience related in this anecdote.

One day, when Plumb and his wife were sitting in a restaurant, a man at another table came up and said, "You're Plumb! You flew jet fighters in Vietnam from the aircraft carrier *Kitty Hawk*. You were shot down!"

"How in the world did you know that?" asked Plumb.

"I packed your parachute," the man replied.

Plumb gasped in surprise and gratitude. The man pumped his hand and said, "I guess it worked!" Plumb assured him, "It sure did. If your chute hadn't worked, I wouldn't be here today."

Plumb couldn't sleep that night, thinking about that man. He said, "I kept wondering what he had looked like in a Navy uniform: a white hat; a bib in the back; and bell-bottom trousers. I wonder how many times I might have seen him and not even said 'Good morning, how are you?' or anything because, you see, I was a fighter pilot and he was just a sailor."

Plumb thought of the many hours the sailor had spent at a long wooden table in the bowels of the ship, carefully weaving the shrouds and folding the silks of each chute, holding in his hands each time the fate of someone he didn't know.

When Plumb relays this story, he always asks his audience, "Who's packing your parachute?"

Everyone has someone who provides what they need to make it through the day. Plumb also points out that he needed many kinds of parachutes when his plane was shot down over enemy territory: he needed his physical parachute, his mental parachute, his emotional parachute and his spiritual parachute. He called on all these supports before reaching safety.

Sometimes in the daily challenges that life gives us, we miss what is really important. We may fail to say *hello, please*, or *thank you*, to congratulate someone on something wonderful that has happened to them, give a compliment, or just do something nice for no reason. As you go through this week, this month, this year, recognize the people who pack your parachutes.[1]

How Do You View People?

How could it be possible that we may overlook the wonderful blessings that certain people bring into our lives, and instead focus our attention on the things that people may do wrong? Do we tend to see the negative in people, rather than the positive? And if so, why? As stated before, "You don't see the world the way the world is; you see the world the way you are." Now we can expand on this concept and say, "You don't see people the way *they* are; you see people the way *you* are."

What does that mean? Quite simply, your personality, prejudices, global beliefs and life experiences will be imprinted upon the interaction you have with every human being with whom you come into contact. If you believe people are generally good, you will see the goodness in them. If you believe they are rotten to the core, then you will see the mistakes they make; in fact, you will focus on those mistakes, highlight them in your mind, delete from your view all of the good that they may do and magnify the faults that you see. Sometimes you will magnify their mistakes past the point of reason. And the entire time, you will believe that your perspective is accurate and your view of the world is sound. You will not realize that you are filtering your experience of people through your own prejudices against them.

Take a moment and consider the following list of characteristics, and try to identify your own beliefs about people.

---

1 Source: www.THAIVISA.com

Generally speaking, people are:

- outgoing   - shy
- leaders   - followers
- organized   - laid back
- responsible   - spontaneous
- self-absorbed   - charitable
- cowardly   - brave

The list can go on and on. You may catch yourself saying, "Generally speaking, the majority of people are foolish and selfish." You may say, "Generally speaking, the majority of people want to do the right thing." What shapes these beliefs? Our experiences, because they have a profound effect upon our belief system. What is amazing is that many times, we do not clearly know which experiences have shaped our worldview; it could have been what our mother and father told us over and over at the dinner table. It could have been what we saw happen to our older brother in the playground. It could have been a story we read in the newspaper about someone else that deeply affected us. Or, most likely, our beliefs came from past experiences (both good and bad) in our relationships with other people. It is extremely important to understand what those experiences are in order to assess their accuracy and see whether or not they contradict other beliefs we hold and to evaluate whether or not they are even fair and rational. If we don't take the time to uncover the defining experiences that shape our beliefs about people, we have little control over our perception of other human beings and the success of our relationships with them.

What Has Shaped Your Beliefs about People?

What are the relationship experiences (both professional and personal) that have shaped your beliefs about people in general? Consider the following situations and generalizations:

- "My Dad always mentioned to the cashier that he had received too much change."

People are honest.

- "My business partner screwed me and stole the money."

Don't trust anyone.

- "My employees slack off when I'm on the road."

People are lazy, and they'll let you down.

- "My employees worked till midnight the last three weeks, and we made our sales."

People are committed.

- "My parents always taught me, 'Watch your back, people will take advantage.'"

People are treacherous.

- "My mother always baked food at the holidays for the less fortunate."

People can show great compassion.

- "My father was a violent alcoholic."

The people you love will hurt you.

- "If the reward is big enough, or the consequence is bad enough, people take action."

Everyone is highly motivated under the right circumstances.

- "My baby girl wandered off at the mall, but a wonderful couple found her for me."

People are generally good.

- "No matter what people do wrong, they each have a genius in some area that I lack."

Everyone can teach you something.

- "I was abandoned at birth, and then adopted by a loving couple."

Some people will betray you, and some people will save you.

- "Thanks to the surgeon, my cancerous tumor has been removed."

People can help others in ways that we think miraculous.

- "A mother and father ran back into their burning home to save their two children."

People are capable of incredible acts of courage.

Once you've identified some of the defining experiences that have shaped your general beliefs about people, ask yourself this: are these beliefs fair? Rational? Do they contradict any of my other beliefs? Do these beliefs serve me well in life, or are they a consistent barrier to health and happy relationships? Is it time to let go of some beliefs I hold?

If you have a thoughtful friend or associate who you regard as successful in personal and professional relationships, you may consider sharing your beliefs with that person. Be particularly curious and open to listening to your friend's perspective, especially her beliefs that differ from yours. Remember, you've selected this person to talk to because you believe that she is successful with relationships. What are your friend's beliefs? Can you hear the story of the experiences that shaped her beliefs and then choose to hang onto that story of her positive experience? Can you allow your friend's positive experiences to soften some of your less tolerant or negative beliefs about people in order to become more effective in relationships with quality people?

It requires great courage, effort and humility to be open to challenging our core beliefs. That's why many individuals never take the time for in introspection. But, you can decide to become a master of personal relationships. Challenge your beliefs and consider letting go of negative beliefs that hold you back from the most rewarding relationships of your life.

What qualities do you look for in
- a spouse/life partner?
- a friendship?
- a business partner/colleague?
- extended family members?

Answering these questions will determine your personal blueprint for relationships. As well, it is important to ask: do I display these qualities? Would I want a friend, spouse or colleague who is like me? What positive qualities do you offer as a friend, spouse or colleague? What qualities would you like to offer people? Finally, is there a difference between who you want to be and who you currently are? Resolve to identify any disparity between your ideal behavior and your current behavior, and take action to grow as an individual.

What qualities of character do you want to offer other people in a relationship with you?

❑ Loyal	❑ Trustworthy
❑ Tolerant	❑ Fair
❑ Humble	❑ Supportive
❑ Fun	❑ Empathetic
❑ Agreeable	❑ Co-operative
❑ Loving	❑ Team-player
❑ Reliable	❑ Leader
❑ Friendly	❑ Kind
❑ Caring	❑ Thankful
❑ Thoughtful	❑ Cheerful
❑ Positive	❑ Sociable

Associate with Winners

Now that you have clarified your ideal blueprint of an effective relationship, you have identified the qualities that you want to offer others in a relationship and revealed the underlying beliefs that shape how you view people. It is time to make an important decision. Possessing knowledge without taking action is useless. Knowing the type of people you desire in your life is not enough; you must resolve to attract that caliber of individual into your life and remove the negative relationships from your life. You must choose to attract winners.

If you've got a relationship that is negative and bringing you down, you need to decide how much time you spend with that person, if any at all. People who become major successes hold themselves and the people around them to a higher standard of excellence. They are quick to sniff out the hidden motives of would-be friends in order to determine sincerity, and they are quick to cast off negative relationships. As a general rule, people who bring you down have no place in your life. This may involve the friend who constantly makes negative remarks about your business or the friend who puts you down when you've made a positive change like losing weight, saving money, getting a promotion, or starting a healthy new relationship. Friends who do not want to personally improve may feel uncomfortable when you do. And they may consciously (or unconsciously) express their displeasure in the form of verbal barbs meant to cut you down and belittle your progress.

Do not tolerate this reprehensible behavior in your life. Make a decision that you will only allow high quality people into your life. This means that people have to qualify to have a relationship with you, and you may need to end certain current relationships. If you have a family member who is consistently insulting your spouse, you may choose to stop associating with that person. If you have a neighbor who is profane and racist in front of your kids, you have a right to cut them off. If your sister cuts you down for going on a diet and losing weight (when she refuses to), spend less time with her.

Admittedly, these may be extreme examples. But do you have relationships that make you feel bad about yourself? That make you feel small, unloved, unwanted or unappreciated? You do not have to tolerate such relationships. Spend less time with people that bring you down. Choose instead to associate with winners.

Establish a Mastermind Group

If I have seen farther than others, it is because I have stood on the shoulders of giants.—Sir Isaac Newton

Winners follow the blueprint of an exceptional relationship. They lift you up, encourage you, catch you doing things right and make you feel great about yourself when life has beaten you up. They stand beside you to make you laugh and offer their shoulder when you need to cry. They lend an ear when you need to talk and give you a hug in celebration of your success. They are not jealous of your progress; they want the very best for you. They make you stronger, smarter and faster than you would be without them. Your life is blessed because of their presence in it.

Make a deliberate decision that you will regularly associate with high quality people. Benjamin Franklin developed a group called the "Junto" to do just that. The group met on Fridays for the purpose of positive association and mutual improvement. The participants discussed morals, politics and philosophy, and took turns researching and writing papers on any subject that interested them. They would meet, read the papers and discuss them together. This group stood the test of time and eventually evolved into the American Philosophical Society, which is still in existence today.

In his immortal work *Think and Grow Rich*, Napoleon Hill describes this fundamental concept as a "Mastermind Group." The basic premise is to make a deliberate decision to collect a small group of exceptional human beings and meet on a regular basis. The purpose of meeting: to improve each individual through association with each person in the group. To hold each individual accountable to his or her dreams and goals. To create synergy. To brainstorm ideas. To challenge each other to grow and improve. To be a foundation of excellence to stand upon when the natural course of events in daily life may prove unsettling. To be positive support in times of challenge, positive encouragement in times of opportunity, to praise and uplift each other, to challenge each other to think big.

Are you part of a mastermind group? You see, those we associate with will contrive to shape our destiny. Motivational speaker Charlie "Tremendous" Jones says, "In five years, two things will determine where you are: the books you read, and the people you associate with." We eventually begin to emulate the behaviors and beliefs of the people we most often spend time with, whether those behaviors and beliefs are good or bad. Take a look at the five people you most often spend time with. Who are they? What is their personal and professional situation like? Are they successful? Are they struggling in one or more areas? How closely do your beliefs mirror theirs? It is very difficult not to adopt the beliefs of the people you spend long periods of time with, so choose those people wisely.

Parents can easily see the effect of association in their children. If your child associates with a child who is rude and uses profanity, do you think there is a chance that your child may come home and share with you some of the new words he or she learned that day? If you know your child is hanging around "bad kids" who are stealing, using drugs, getting involved in violence or any other negative behavior, do you want your children associating with them? Of course not. Why? Because you are concerned that your children will begin to pick up those bad behaviors and beliefs.

It is amazing that we realize the power of association and how it affects our children, yet we are quick to forget how association affects us as adults! You are the people you associate with. If you hang around pessimistic people, their negative thinking will eventually seep into your mind. If you hang around with people who belittle you and point out why you are weak, stupid, incompetent or inferior, you risk believing what they say. The only way to effectively combat their poisonous words is to avoid them altogether. Choose the people you spend time with very carefully. Choose to form a mastermind group with individuals of the highest caliber, and associate with winners on a regular basis.

Develop Your People Skills

Relating to people with ease is often difficult for most of us, yet it is an extremely valuable skill that has a lot to do with our desire to succeed. Are you adept at motivating people? Do you come across as genuine and understanding? Find out how important the trust factor is.

Can You Improve Your Skills in Relationships?

The short answer is *yes*, if you are committed to learning the art of working and living well with people. Since so much of the quality of our lives is affected by the quality of our relationships, anyone with a passion for life can recognize that interacting well with others needs to be a top priority. If you've struggled with effectiveness in relationships before, the door has not yet closed on the possibility of becoming more skilled. The ability to connect with people is a skill that comes naturally for some people, but not having natural social skills does not bar you from learning the art of people skills. For people who are good at relationships, it's like the natural-born talent that some people have for playing a musical instrument; they don't know how they play so well, they just do. For those individuals who are naturally charismatic and skilled with people, they can probably get by without ever getting better. People who don't have this natural ability have to develop this skill because social interaction is so important in life and business. Studying the skills of human interaction and practicing these skills can make you more effective in all areas of life. With study, practice and discipline, you can become proficient at these fundamental skills.

The Foundation of Good People Skills

1. Practice Integrity.

Exceptional people skills stem first and foremost from being an exceptional person. Your integrity is the long-term report card on your value to others. Building a reputation of the highest ethics and standards is the best introduction to any room you enter. Keep the confidence of the people who have trusted you with their secrets, keep the respect of those who depend upon your good judgment and honor the commitments you have made by performing to the best of your ability at all times. All of the flash, shiny veneer and people skills in the world won't make up for a history of breaking your word and letting people down. Establish and maintain an impeccable code of conduct. Wear integrity like your coat-of-arms, and do what you say you will do.

2. Fill Your Emotional Bank Account.

Treat people well. Be respectful and considerate in your dealings with others. If you treat people badly, the history of your negative behavior will plague all of your interactions with them in the future. At all times, your reputation is on the line. Recognize that life accumulates. You can't be rude to someone, treat them poorly and expect them to forgive you because you pretend to be nice only when you need a favor from them. You can't succeed in the long run by using people skills to manipulate people. Turning on the false charm at the 11th hour doesn't have any impact if you've been disrespectful and built a reputation of shallow manipulation and deceit.

3. Feel Good about Yourself.

People are attracted to self-assured people. False bravado will not hide a weakened confidence in yourself for long. If you don't like yourself, it's going to be an uphill battle for other people to feel differently. People with low self-esteem will deflect the compliments shared in conversation. When someone compliments them on an award they won, a person with low self-esteem will say, "Oh, it's not that special." Feel proud of your gifts, your strengths and know in your heart the tremendous value you have to offer the world. People will feel that self-esteem coming through in your actions and speech.

4. Get Interested in Other People.

If you can see the beauty in other human beings, you won't need to invest in fake personality skills training and people-manipulation techniques that some books expound. The reason? You won't need to feign affection for other people; you will genuinely like them. All people have something special about them. Everyone has talents and skills that remain hidden from view when we first meet him or her. The cab driver holds a PhD in chemistry from another country. The maid scrubbing your floors never went to school but saved enough money to send her daughter to college for a better life. The school teacher has saved a dozen children from joining street gangs. The chemist is a brilliant husband and has enjoyed a life-long romance with his wife. The junior law clerk has the voice of an angel and she stops the hearts of every member of her congregation at church when she sings. The CEO of a technology firm devotes two Saturdays a month to spending time at an orphanage, reading stories and playing with the kids there in order to show them that they are loved. Everyone has a story we don't know. Get interested in the hidden beauty within every person.

Basic Skills

1. Smile.

This is the first and most basic of people skills. A smile tells people that you are friendly, that you like them, that they are safe with you and that you are interested in connecting with them. A smile is the best fashion accessory you can wear to make yourself more attractive. But beware: don't smile too quickly, don't smile disingenuously and be sure that it doesn't become the wallpaper on your face. If you keep a perma-smile plastered on your lips, it begins to lack credibility. Smile when you've got a good reason, not because you think you should. Smile when you feel happy, when you find something funny, when you see a friend, when you want to share your happiness with others you pass during the day.

2. Make and Keep Eye Contact.

But be sure that it is something that makes the other person feel good. Generally, eye contact is positive and shows a healthy self-confidence. It may be perceived as you showing interest in the other person. But be aware that a shy person might feel that you are staring at them. To individuals from some cultures, it may appear that you are staring them down aggressively in a confrontational or disrespectful way.

3. Extend Genuine Compliments.

Notice that this point does not say to merely compliment people, but rather to genuinely compliment people. Look for the good in people; everyone has something positive about themselves, something that they are good at. Don't offer false flattery and say that you like something that you don't; duplicity will detract from your integrity.

4. Remember People's Names.

As Dale Carnegie said in *How to Win Friends and Influence People,* "A person's name is the sweetest and most important sound in any language." Recognize what remembering someone's name says to that person: it means that they are important enough to you to remember them. It is one of the highest general compliments you can offer people. To mistake a person's name is slightly offsetting and can even be offensive, particularly when the person has repeated it for you several times. When you meet someone, always offer your name, and make sure that you have heard the name of the person you're meeting. Repeat his or her name out loud to further solidify your memory of it: "David? Hi David, nice to meet you!"

You may choose to strengthen the memory of a name in your mind by thinking of someone else with the same name. Visualize both of their faces, and then in your mind's eye you can merge their faces, thereby connecting the name to the face. If a name reminds you of an object or item, try connecting the name to the image in your mind. If a name is unusual to you, you might say gently, "Sorry, I didn't catch your name; could you help me learn to pronounce it correctly please?" Repeat the name back to ensure that you clearly understand it. Repeat the person's name a few times in conversation, and be sure to repeat the name when you say hello. When you learn people's names, they feel that you have taken a genuine interest in them, and your stock in their eyes will rise!

5. Talk about What Other People Find Interesting.
The reason? Because you find them interesting, and you find their passions interesting as well. Perhaps you don't like hockey; can you feel happy for someone who is excited about the big game that night? Perhaps you are not Christian. Can you get excited because your dear friend is getting baptized, and it's important to him? Can you develop a fascination with the world around you and take a keen interest in people? That is genuine. As well, you can offer others the opportunity to share a story about themselves. Many people feel that they are the most interesting subject and can't wait to talk about themselves! They might think you are the best conversationalist in the world because you listened intently to the stories they regaled you with about their adventures.

Building Rapport
Rapport opens the door to a relationship. Rapport is the art of connecting with a person upon first meeting. It's that feeling that you both like each other and will enjoy talking together. Some people go to the extreme when attempting to build rapport by acting completely different from their true personality in order to get the other person to like them. Rapport doesn't mean changing your personality; it means bringing out the qualities in your personality that are most similar to the person you are talking with. Rapport is the absence of awareness of difference; it is a positive connection between people that makes them feel "I like this person."

Here are some techniques for learning to build rapport with others.

1. Take the Initiative to Introduce Yourself.
Be the one to extend your hand, to chit-chat and initiate conversation. Most people shy away from the initial contact because they risk rejection when they initiate. Be courageous in your

interaction with people. Stretch your comfort zone and push yourself to engage in situations that are less comfortable; doing what is uncomfortable will force you to grow. In time, the discomfort you may have initially felt is replaced with confidence. What would it mean to be able to walk into a room of strangers with confidence and leave having made new friends and potential contacts? Take action and say hello.

2. Stand and Move with Confidence.
Ask yourself, "If I were an actor in a movie and I had to play the confident hero, how would I stand? What about my posture? Would I look up? Would I hold my shoulders back? Have an expression of confidence? Walk 25 percent faster, like someone who was on a mission and had somewhere important to go?"

People will form an opinion of you within the first few seconds based largely on how you look, including your clothing, the expression on your face and your posture. Show them in the first few seconds that you believe in yourself, that you are a person worth knowing, that you offer tremendous value to the world and that you fully realize you are a worthwhile human being. People are attracted to people who have a healthy self-esteem. Show it in your posture.

3. Use Open Body Language.
Before you say a single word, people are sizing you up and asking themselves one question: Do I like this person? As mentioned before, smiling is a foundational people skill because it immediately communicates to most people that you are friendly, trustworthy, safe to connect with and interested in connecting. And smiling achieves this without you having to say a single word. You can back up the positive impact of your smile with open body language. By keeping your arms uncrossed or your

jacket unbuttoned, you show that you are approachable. This does not mean that if you are talking to someone and he crosses his arms this means he disagrees with or doesn't like you. While that is possible, it may just mean that he is physically more comfortable crossing his arms; perhaps he is sitting in a chair without arm rests or he's cold.

But be aware that you may be sending an erroneous signal if your arms are crossed for an innocent reason; the person you are talking to may mistake your body language for meaning you don't like her. Notice if your hands are closed in a fist, if your jaw is clenched, brows furrowed or if your eyes have narrowed and tightened. Consider modifying your stance if you think you might be making people ill at ease. You may even say, "I don't disagree with you; I've got my arms crossed because it's more comfortable for me."

4. Mirror Body Language.
People form relationships (and subsequently, do business with) people that they know, like and trust. We simply like people more who are more like us. People tend to gravitate towards people who are similar to them with similar interests, a similar belief system, similar tastes in fashion, similar hobbies or a similar personality. So, you can also set people at ease and become a master of building rapport by adopting their body language for a short period of time. Simply put, if the person you are interacting with is leaning forward, you may choose to lean forward. If she is standing confidently, you may do the same. If she is tapping her foot, you may choose to tap your fingers with the same rhythm.

Why would you do this? Because unconsciously, people will feel that you are similar at some level. If you are subtle with your mirroring and don't act like you are playing "Simon Says" by copying every single gesture, she will find that she feels at ease with you. If you engage in the opposite body language, she may feel that there just isn't as strong a connection between the two of you, and she may be slightly put off. If she is leaning forward with interest and you are slouched back with your feet up on the table, she may take that to mean that you are disinterested in what she has to say. But if she is leaning back with her feet up and you match her stance by doing the same, she might feel, "Hey, this is someone like me; someone I can trust and get to know."

Learn to Understand Personalities

Every successful leader knows that a team is made up of people with different strengths. No winning football team could be made up entirely of quarterbacks. This would invite disaster. You'll need a linebacker, wide receiver, halfback, and defensive end, among others, to win your game. Similarly, no relationship, family, corporation or organization will flourish with only one type of personality filling the ranks.

In your corporation, you will need outgoing and confident salespeople, friendly and agreeable customer service agents, supportive and organized warehouse and maintenance staff, and analytical accountants and information technology staff. You will need leaders and followers and both people-oriented and task-oriented individuals. In your family, one person could be good at organizing the bank statements and managing the money. Someone else could be good at injecting the warmth, spontaneity and fun into social events. Another could be the gentle and flexible peacekeeper, and someone could make the big decisions and bear responsibility for bringing home the bacon. The most successful businesses, families and relationships will mix together a group of people who bring a variety of different strengths and talents to the table, thereby ensuring that the group can handle any situation that occurs.

However, many times we only want to attract people who are like us: if we are outgoing, we may prefer to work with only outgoing people. If we are a leader, we may only want to work with "take action and defeat the enemy" type of people. If we are highly organized and methodical, we may not like working with someone who is messy; but that messy person may be cheerful and engaging, making all of your guests and clients feel warm and welcome. Everyone has his or her own unique personality, with strengths as well as weaknesses. One of the greatest discoveries of your life may occur when you realize that the person with whom you don't get along actually has a strength that you are lacking—and desperately require. If you can see the wonderful gifts that people bring to the table, rather than liking or disliking them based upon their similarity to you, you will lay the foundation for building a winning team with a diverse range of strengths.

So, what are the strengths and weaknesses of the people in your personal and professional life? What gifts do they have? Let's take a few moments and discuss a model of human behavior that is simple and effective at revealing the strengths that various personalities have to offer. In doing so, you may better understand the people around you, and you may even more clearly understand yourself.

A Model of Human Behavior

People don't like to be labeled or put in a box, but if we can understand some general principles about human behavior and personality structure, we will have a starting point to better understand the people around us—and to understand ourselves! There are four basic personality styles, and everyone has some of each. Most importantly, everyone has a clearly dominant and a secondary style. Your dominant personality style will direct how you relate to others (and how you would prefer that they relate to you). Being able to recognize your dominant personality trait (and that of others) helps you to be more effective in working with people because you understand better their strengths, motivations, and limitations. In order to understand personalities, let's imagine that we divide a piece of pie into different sections.

We'll start with understanding if someone is …

Outgoing versus Reserved

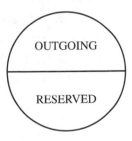

The first quality of character in determining personality styles is someone's level of interpersonal engagement: is the person more outgoing or more reserved? On one side of the coin, a person may be talkative, energetic, moving with confidence and commanding attention when they walk into a room. We could label them as "outgoing." On the other side, a person might be more of a "turtle" than a "hare" and move and talk more slowly, approaching life more cautiously. They might be the wallflower in the room … and we might call them "reserved."

Task-Oriented versus People-Oriented

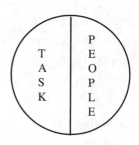

The second quality of character in determining personality styles is someone's interpersonal focus: are they more interested in people, or are they more interested in getting work done? If someone seems more empathetic about others' feelings, and looks forward to socializing with friends and family, we might call them more "people-oriented." If going to a party is akin to pulling their hair out, and they would rather accomplish a goal or finish work than hang around socializing, we might call them more "task-oriented."

Put it all together ...

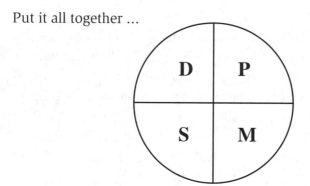

Director: Outgoing and task-oriented, these individuals' motto is "my way, or the highway!" They are often the general of their own little army. While they may get the task accomplished, they might do so by being pushy and offending people.

Presenter: Outgoing and people-oriented, these individuals can't wait to get to the next party! They love being around people, make friends easily, and love to be the center of attention. Sometimes, though, they can be disorganized and miss details.

Mediator: Reserved and people-oriented, these individuals want to stay in the background and help you have your moment of success. Very sweet, sometimes shy, and they can't say *no*!

Strategist: Reserved and task-oriented, strategists are the accountants, the engineers, the perfectionists, who are focused on accuracy and excellence. They enjoy balancing their checkbooks more than going to a party and can sometimes be cold and unemotional.

Personality Style Self-Analysis

Take a moment to clarify which personality style might be your most dominant. In each column, check off the words that describe you, and add up your results! For example, if you score 18 under "Director," 12 under "Presenter," 6 under "Mediator" and 2 under "Strategist," then your Dominant style is "Director" and your secondary style is "Presenter."

DIRECTOR
- ❏ Visionary
- ❏ Forceful
- ❏ Achieving
- ❏ Decisive
- ❏ Focused
- ❏ Courageous
- ❏ Likes a challenge
- ❏ Determined
- ❏ Gutsy
- ❏ Daring
- ❏ Bold
- ❏ Aggressive
- ❏ Driven
- ❏ Wants to win
- ❏ Unyielding
- ❏ Risk-Taking
- ❏ Adventurous
- ❏ Decision-maker
- ❏ Competitive
- ❏ Assertive

Total: _____

PRESENTER
- ❏ Fun
- ❏ Likeable
- ❏ Lively
- ❏ Upbeat
- ❏ Excitable
- ❏ Animated
- ❏ Makes friends easily
- ❏ Sociable
- ❏ Personable
- ❏ Big-hearted
- ❏ Likes to talk
- ❏ Expressive
- ❏ Dramatic
- ❏ Life of the party
- ❏ Likes attention
- ❏ Cheerful
- ❏ Restless
- ❏ Easily bored
- ❏ Popular
- ❏ Emotive

Total: _____

STRATEGIST
- ❏ Evaluating
- ❏ Methodical
- ❏ Attentive to details
- ❏ Calculating
- ❏ Analytical
- ❏ Observant
- ❏ Careful

MEDIATOR
- ❏ Kind
- ❏ Softhearted
- ❏ Sweet
- ❏ Supportive
- ❏ Pleasant
- ❏ Warm
- ❏ Faithful

❑ Cautious
❑ Specific
❑ Exact
❑ Correct
❑ Particular
❑ Modest
❑ Anxious
❑ Apprehensive
❑ Private
❑ Subdued
❑ Appropriate
❑ Tactful
❑ Weighs Risks

❑ Steadfast
❑ Willing to help
❑ Thoughtful
❑ Relaxed
❑ Content
❑ Not excitable
❑ Agreeable
❑ Devoted
❑ Submits easily
❑ Accommodating
❑ Considerate of others
❑ Loyal
❑ Patient

Total: _____

Total: _____

Director—Outgoing and Task-Oriented

Visionary

Directors are able to see the big picture. They don't allow details to slow them down from seeing the greater possibilities. They see possibility, opportunity and make grandiose connections in their mind. They will begin the adventure and figure out what they need along the way. They have a sense of confidence that things will turn out for the best, and their visionary charisma tends to turn the tides in their favor. They think big, believe big and their actions are bold and audacious. Because of this, Directors are frequently in positions of leadership.

Focused

Directors can be single-minded in their action, pursuing the prize on which they have affixed their gaze. Whereas other people may be distracted by minutia, Directors are most likely to keep the proverbial blinders on and finish the race ahead of the pack.

Achieving
Directors are Olympic goal-setting animals; they go after what they want and get it. Directors don't spend a lot of time sitting on the couch watching life pass them by. Life doesn't happen to a Director; a Director happens to life. Their list of conquests and victories is usually long and distinguished. Directors get the job done.

Competitive
In the Director's mind, the second-place medal is actually the first-place medal for losers. For example, Michael Jordan is renowned for his fiercely competitive spirit; when his basketball teammates beat him at ping-pong on their time off, Michael hired a world-class ping-pong coach to train him to become the best. He would not allow himself to be second place in anything.

Decisive
In the words of Tom Peters, Directors have "a bias for action." Directors make decisions quickly and may be slow to change their mind about decisions once made. They would rather press on through difficulty than throw in the towel. However, when the situation calls for it, they can effortlessly turn on a dime and adopt a new direction of attack, shrugging off the old way of doing things without a moment's hesitation. They don't care about how to get to victory; if they can't go around the brick wall, they will build a door or knock down the wall with explosives.

Courageous
Directors will take action even with great opposition. In fact, sometimes the best way to motivate Directors is to tell them that

you don't think they are capable of doing something. They might just do it, simply to prove you wrong. "I can't" is incomprehensible to a Director. They are highly self-reliant and won't wait for a handout from the world. The greater the odds against them, the more they relish the chance to get in the fight.

Motivators
Directors want power, control, action, challenge, big-picture thinking, the bottom line and boldness.

Weaknesses
Directors are unforgiving of weakness or poor performance in others. They tend to be blunt and run over people's feelings. Often, they are either unaware they are doing this or unsympathetic to the sensitivities of others. Because of this, they may rub people the wrong way and upset other team members.

Presenter—Outgoing and People-Oriented
Outgoing
There isn't a shy bone in a presenter. Presenters will say "hi" to people on the elevator, strike up a conversation with the cab driver and comment on the vegetables of the person beside them in the grocery store checkout line. They have no problem getting up and speaking before a large crowd; in fact, they can hardly sit still if they're in the audience. They love the spotlight and relish having all of the eyes of the room on them. They are the high school prom queens, cheerleaders, MCs, and they are most certainly their own favorite person.

Fun
Presenters are the life of the party! In fact, many times they *are* the party. They can brighten a room when they walk in. Whenever

you see a crowd gathering, you can bet that they are either the center of attention, or clamoring to share in the excitement. They might be the class clown or the office prankster. You can count on them to liven things up a bit. They can lack the ability to have an internal dialogue, and sometimes figure things out by talking about it and hearing their own voice. They tend to blurt things out without considering the consequences, so it can be just as entertaining to listen to find out what they're going to say next.

Great Networkers

Presenters feel that strangers are simply friends that they haven't met yet. Outgoing and people-oriented, presenters make initial connections more easily than other people. Whereas other people may have to work up the courage to go shake hands with someone "important," presenters have already pushed their way to the front of the crowd to make their introduction. They can make a big, loud, memorable impression in a short period of time.

High Energy

Presenters are dynamic, engaging and full of life. They don't want to sit still, they want to move and talk and experience what life has to offer. They jump from one thing to the next with zest. If something's happening, they want to be involved: who's there, where is it happening, when is it going down?

Dramatic

Things are always bigger, brighter, and more exciting whenever presenters tell the story. The fish they caught was the biggest *ever*. The restaurant they had lunch at has the best food. The movie they saw Saturday was their *favorite movie ever*. The rock concert was the *most amazing they've ever gone to*. This summer's vacation was the *most fun ever*. Their new business venture will be their *biggest success*. The slightest setback they face is an *absolute disaster*. Any progress they make is a *monumental achievement*. For a presenter, everything is magnified and bigger than life.

Motivators
They want to be in the spotlight, the star of the show, have fun, be with people and get the credit.

Weaknesses
Details bore them quickly and they will lose interest. They may exaggerate details or even make them up, not realizing the need for accuracy in many situations. They tend to be disorganized, and over-commit to projects, not realizing that they've already made other commitments. They lack focus and jump from one thing to the next. They tend to hog the credit and the spotlight. In their mind, it's all about them. They are weaker with follow-up skills.

Mediator—Reserved and People-Oriented
Supportive
The mediator wants to help other people reach their own personal goals and dreams. Mediators can be very selfless and giving to others, sometimes at their own expense. Their focus is you, and how they can help you. They don't want the spotlight; they want to be in the background and let you have the credit. They will look for ways to go the extra mile in the name of you or the team. Making people feel cared for and satisfied is one of their greatest pleasures. Whenever you need someone to lean on, a mediator will drive through a blizzard at 3 a.m. in order to help out.

Loyal
A mediator will stay by your side until the very end. They are the last person who would break your confidence. You can count

on them. They are fiercely dependable. A football team can only have one quarterback, and an army needs only one general. Mediators are the masses of foot soldiers who happily and loyally want to help the people they love get the big job done, and few leaders can achieve greatly without a strong team of mediators behind them.

Great Finishers
Mediators are like the turtle racing the hare: they are slow to start, they move gradually towards the finish line, but they methodically make progress until eventually completing the task at hand. They finish what they start—especially if someone is counting on them.

Easy-going
Nothing seems to ruffle their feathers. Their motto is "Whatever you want is fine with me." They are gentle in their mannerisms, speech and body language, never wanting to appear pushy or aggressive. In fact, being around a mediator may even have a calming effect on more high-strung personalities. Rarely do they raise their voice. It takes a long time for them to boil over in anger; in fact, most anger is usually expressed in passive-aggressive behavior with them avoiding any type of direct confrontation.

Agreeable
Mediators tend to get along with people more effectively than any other personality. They're some of the sweetest, nicest people you know. They are warm, flexible and compassionate. It is extremely important to them to keep the peace and make sure that everyone is getting along. They'll do anything not to rock the boat, even if it means giving up what they personally want in order to let someone else get their way.

Considerate
Mediators always think about how their actions will make other people feel. They are perhaps the most empathetic of all person-alities and extremely skilled at reading the emotions of other people; this is due in part because it is a high priority for them. They quickly notice if someone else is feeling upset, discouraged, anxious or sad. They genuinely desire making the other person feel better. They want to make others happy and look to see if their actions have soothed tensions or lifted spirits.

Motivators
Keeping the peace, helping others, being kind, getting along with everyone. They like keeping the status quo and things they way they are.

Weaknesses
They tend to be taken advantage of, don't stand up for them-selves and struggle with setting clear boundaries in relationships and saying *no*. They avoid confrontation at all costs, even if confrontation is necessary and would be healthy in the long run. They can react poorly to change and wish things were the way they used to be.

Strategist—Reserved and Task-Oriented
Capable
Strategists know what they are doing. They are often highly skilled and experienced professionals with a wealth of training knowledge at their fingertips. They may have spent years in school and in the field honing their craft and they know exactly what they are doing. They gravitate towards careers that demand a high intellect and precision, such as engineering, medicine, finance, science, computer technology and aerospace. Strategists

include the neurosurgeon removing a tumor, the military demolitions expert who lays the explosives to bring down the enemy bridge, the scientist working with DNA. When it comes to the job at hand, you can trust them to get it right.

Precise
Strategists value accuracy above all else. They are neat, orderly and exact in their work and life. You don't need to check their work to see if it's correct; they've already checked it three times themselves. They won't hand you anything that they aren't certain is correct. They dot the *i*'s, cross the *t*'s, triple-check the bankbook, follow procedures to the letter and crosscheck the test results. They don't wing it, play it by ear, guess or take their best shot. They struggle with people who want to fly by the seat of their pants.

Consistent
Strategists enjoy routine and habitual patterns. They are slower to change because they have already discovered what works for them. They are far more predictable than other people. Their motto is often "If it isn't broken, don't fix it." Their schedules are highly structured. They might buy five suits and shirts that are the same because it's more efficient to not have to think about clothing each day. They don't like surprises; they want everything planned in advance to the letter.

Clear-Thinking
Strategists are able to consider the details of the situation with little or no emotion. They are extremely clever at solving logistical problems. They are highly adept at keeping their cool while others are losing theirs. They see the solutions to problems quickly because they can retain vast amounts of data and information in their active memory. They won't leap before looking, and

this serves them and their team well because it helps to avoid potential mistakes by "fools who rush in."

Motivators
Demanding nothing short of accuracy; using their expertise and intelligence to tackle tough challenges.

Weaknesses
Because they are highly skilled and intelligent in some areas, they mistakenly assume that they are always right in every area. They can be intellectual snobs and dismiss others who are not as experienced as they are. Strategists can pursue perfection to the point of paralysis. They tend to be more pessimistic, critical and negative than other personalities. They may look at what is wrong with a situation more often than what is right, ignoring the 99 percent that is wonderful and focusing on the 1 percent blemish. Because of their critical nature, they are very hard on themselves when they make mistakes and can be very sensitive to criticism about accuracy and their knowledge.

Seeing the Value in Different Personality Types
As you can see, every personality type has its own unique strengths and weaknesses. Of the four types we've just discussed (director, presenter, mediator, and strategist), which one most closely describes you? Understand that every person is a blend of all four personality types, just in different degrees. You will exhibit one personality type more strongly than the others, followed by a secondary type and a tertiary type. Understanding people's motivations, strengths and weaknesses is the key to assembling effective and successful teams!

Interestingly, it is very likely that the person you relate to least is the person who is extremely good at the one thing you struggle with the most. This is the paradox of building effective teams, families and organizations: you don't want an army of clones. You want a quarterback, linebacker, fullback and every other strength you can recruit. You may not like Yolanda because she is so soft and gentle, but maybe she is better at dealing with people. You may not like Dave because he is argumentative and pushy, but he has the confidence to walk into a room of investors and make a confident pitch to raise capital. You may not like Carla because she is so cold and nit-picky, but thank goodness she keeps your operations running like a well-oiled machine. You may not like Alan because he is always chatty and seems superficial and disorganized, but he is certainly a people magnet. Whenever he walks into the room, the whole place lights up.

You see, the person we don't connect with might hold the secret to us graduating to the next level of success in our personal and professional life, if we are humble and open to learning the lessons that they may offer.

Building Rapport by Understanding Personalities

Can understanding personality types assist you in creating rapport with people? Absolutely! Think of how important it is when discussing an idea with someone if you could know whether she would prefer that you get to the point quickly, or explain all of the details in minutia. What if she likes to talk fast? It might make sense that she would prefer to listen fast as well, and want you to emulate them. What if she is slow to make decisions and you are pressuring her to decide quickly? It helps to know if this is a turn-off for her personality type.

So, how can you use your understanding of personality types to build rapport? Identify a person's personality style and adapt your approach. Pay attention to peoples' body language, tone of voice, and the words and ideas they share. Try to determine if they are more outgoing or reserved, and if they are more people-oriented or more task-oriented.

a. **Is this person a reserved type?**

You can see this by looking to see if he glances down shyly, seems to be standing like a wallflower at the edge of the room, or meekly moves around people without engaging them. Does he speak so softly it's hard to hear him, and does he seem almost apologetic as he speaks? Is his voice soft and monotone? Are his body movements reserved in nature? This might indicate a reserved person.

b. **Is this person the outgoing type?**

Does she speak loudly, quickly, more passionately? Does she use big, expressive gestures? Is she animated? Does she have trouble sitting still? Does she engage people with confidence and have no problem walking up to others to strike up a conversation? Does she move and sound like she has energy?

c. **Is this person people-oriented?**

If so, he will want to be around other people. He will want to talk to people about people. People's reactions and feelings will be important to him. Does he seem more caring of others? Does he seem to care what others think about him? Does he like to chit-chat without purpose, or visit with friends with no set agenda?

d. **Is this person task-oriented?**

If so, she will want to be doing something. Socializing is akin to punishment. She will want to talk about work, about the objective, about accomplishing something. If she is at a party, she will want to be more involved in the logistics of running the show rather than socializing and engaging in conversation.

As you more clearly identify people's personality styles, simply accentuate the side of your personality that is most like them. Don't fake that you are something that you are not; everyone has a little of each style in them. But if you are talking to a **Mediator**, you might overwhelm him by slapping him on the back and loudly proclaiming, "Hey Buddy! How the heck are you?" while pumping his hand vigorously in a handshake. He won't like the aggressiveness and the attention. Try softening your tone and being considerate; he may be shy.

If you are dealing with a **Presenter**, her favorite subject is herself; be sure to genuinely compliment her and let her have the spotlight. Who, where, why and with whom is most interesting to her. Fun and lighthearted banter is the name of the game.

A **Director** wants to get the job done. If getting the job done means schmoozing with clients, so be it. The Director is the Alpha Male in the pack, and probably expects that you recognize that fact and act with appropriate respect of his power and influence. He will have a strong, commanding presence and bigger, louder actions and tone.

To a **Strategist**, socializing can be an awkward and highly uncomfortable situation. The last thing he wants to do is socialize and talk about people. If he has to be at the party, he wants to talk about the latest data, the figures that have just crossed his desk, how the new computer network is standing up in the lab tests and how the dollar is performing against international business. He tends to be emotionless and speak in a monotone.

Individuals of each personality type have their own body language, tone of voice, words and ideas that appeal to them. Identifying the other person's style and modifying your approach might make you the hit of the party, a welcome addition to your fiancées family, or the best closer on your sales team.

Summary

Passionate relationships serve to encourage and energize us, synergize others' efforts and ideas with ours, and make our life greater than it was without them. If you haven't yet done so, make the resolution that you will place a higher priority on the key relationships in your life. Having poor relationship skills may drive away the most important people in your life. It may drive away key partners who would lend their talents to helping you achieve your dreams. It may drive away the loved ones who will make achieving your goals feel worthwhile. Every person who enters your life has the capacity to encourage and lift you one rung higher on the ladder to your dreams and goals, and presents you with the same opportunity to lift them.

You must choose to model the types of behaviours that you would want others to offer you in a relationship. You must extend yourself and make the first connection, catch someone's eye with a smile and extend your hand in greeting. Resolve that you will make people feel welcome and invite them to come in from the cold of the world by the hearth of your personhood, to warm their hands with the heat of your love and caring for them. Decide at all times to see the very best in people, to recognize their strengths and celebrate them, realizing that we are all unique and all uniquely special.

In the end, it all comes down to relationships. A vibrant and loving family is a collection of vibrant and loving people. The greatest asset a corporation has is its people. And in all interactions, we have the opportunity to drive people away or draw them to us like a magnet. Are you attractive, literally attractive, to quality people? If not, what is it costing you in your personal and professional life?

Mastering the art of building and maintaining effective relationships will unlock doors that may have remained closed to you and reveal a path to riches that will offer dividends for a lifetime to come. Make the pursuit of passionate relationships in your life a priority.

Action Steps

1. What are your beliefs about people? How do you view people? What childhood experiences shaped your beliefs about people and relationships? Generally speaking, people are…

2. What qualities of character do *you* want to offer others in relationship with you? Identify your "rough edges" and work on them.

3. Form a Mastermind Group. Choose to associate with winners. Identify five people in your life with whom you would like to nurture a closer relationship. Reach out to them in order to connect.

4. Do you emulate effective people skills? Watch your behavior over the coming days and weeks to see if you are upholding the basic principles we have discussed.

5. Identify your personality type. Identify the personality type for your closest family, friends and colleagues. Which personality type are you and your circle and what strengths does each person bring to the table? What are their weaknesses? Their motivators?

4

financial mastery

> Wishing will not bring riches. But desiring riches with a state of mind that becomes an obsession, then planning definite ways and means to acquire riches, and backing those plans with persistence which does not recognize failure, will bring riches.
>
> —Napoleon Hill, *Think and Grow Rich*

Have you selected your career based upon playing it safe rather than asking yourself, "What would I love to do?"

You're not alone. People do this out of a fear-based mentality, rather than utilizing an abundance-based Wealth Blueprint. Perhaps they heard their parents scoff at their career choice, saying, "You'll never make it doing that. You should get a nice, safe and secure job, working for a big company that will take care of you." After a few disappointments and setbacks, many people throw in the towel on pursuing their passion, if they even had the courage to go after it in the first place.

It is incredibly difficult to become wealthy doing something you aren't passionate about. And if you do, it will be difficult to prolong. You won't have the energy to sustain yourself when the chips are down and you have to work all night to finish a major project or meet a deadline. Passion will fuel your energy when you face crushing setbacks. It will strengthen your resolve when other people put you down and say, "You won't make it!"

The wealthiest people in the world do what they are passionate about. Donald Trump is passionate about real estate development. Bill Gates is passionate about creating software and improving our world. Oprah Winfrey is passionate about reaching millions of people with a positive message. Steven Spielberg is passionate about making movies.

Dreamers don't wait for all of their ducks to be lined up in a row. They don't wait for providence to move in their favor before embarking on a daring adventure. They go after their dreams with passion. They create opportunity. However, they are also shrewd and balanced in making bold decisions. It makes no sense to quit a six-figure job that you are bored with if you haven't yet done the hard work of creating a plan to succeed with your passion. There is a difference between taking positive action to defeat procrastination versus taking foolishly destructive action that leaves you in financial ruin.

Dreamers who succeed have combined their passion with a plan for wealth creation. They combine the first principle of goal setting with the fourth principle of financial mastery. They ask, "How can I make money doing what I love?" This is one of the most important questions you can ask yourself. It forces your mind to look for solutions, to see possibilities that others may miss, to reveal opportunities in the midst of setbacks and disappointments. People who truly desire wealth realize that the pathway to massive wealth lies in the successful pursuit of their dreams. They also realize that, no matter how passionate you are, if you don't understand the principles of wealth creation, you will never attract and retain great sums of money. You must also unlock the secrets of creating great sums of money. And so, let's begin.

Why Don't More People Become Wealthy?

Most people struggle with achieving their financial desires. If you were to ask the average person on the street what would solve his or her financial problems, he or she would likely answer getting a raise at work. If she is earning $40,000, she believes that all of her financial problems would be solved if she could just earn $50,000. If he is making $80,000, he thinks that his problems would be solved if he could just make $100,000. If she's making $400,000, she longs to make $500,000. And the guy making $20,000 dreams of making $25,000. Most people think that making more money will solve their financial problems, and they couldn't be more wrong.

People are constantly thinking of ways to get more money to solve their money problems. In fact, the most popular ways of (legally) getting money are:

1. Getting a raise at work
2. Receiving an inheritance
3. Suing someone and winning
4. Marrying into money
5. Winning the lottery

Have you ever heard stories of people winning the lottery and what they did with the money? The happy couple, when asked by interviewers, "What will you do with the money?" usually exclaim, "We're going on vacation, we're buying a mansion and some fancy cars, and then we're going shopping!" These people think that their money problems are over; after all, they've won the lottery, right? Wrong! The average lottery winner ends up spending the money entirely within a matter of years. Very rarely do they manage their money well, and even rarer still are those who grow the money. Why is this? If the challenge in life for most people is that they don't have enough money, then lottery winners would stay rich. However, the truth is much simpler but harder to change. The number one reason that more people don't become wealthy is simply that they do not think like a wealthy person.

Once we accept the reality of this assertion, the next question is, "How does a wealthy person think, and how can I learn to think the same way?" Let's investigate this concept fully by discussing:

1.   the basics of sound financial management
2.   the money beliefs of wealthy people
3.   how to identify your "money blueprint" and create empowering beliefs
4.   immediate action steps to realize your financial goals.

Financial Management 101

By reading and acting on the concepts in this book, chances are that you are committed to mastering all facets of your life and enjoying great prosperity. What follows is a summary of some fundamental principles of money management and wealth creation. You may be familiar with some or all of these principles and feel that you don't need to review these ideas. Consider this section a self-diagnostic checkup. It is one thing to know what you should do, and quite another to actually do it. While you are reviewing these fundamental principles, ask yourself: "Am I doing all of these things correctly or to my best ability?" If not, this is the time to correct your course. In his book *Success Is Not an Accident*, Tommy Newbury says, "There is nothing more dangerous to your future success than assuming that you're good at a critical skill when your knowledge is rudimentary at best." Therefore, let's approach reviewing these fundamentals with enthusiasm! They are:

- Pay yourself *first*.
- Live beneath your means.
- Don't pay for expenses on credit—pay cash.
- Buy assets, not expenses.
- Don't work for money; make money work for you.
- Strategically reduce debt.
- Make compound interest work for you.

1. Pay Yourself First

Whether you are an employee, self-employed professional or business owner, the first person you must pay each time you get a paycheck is *you*. Why? Because you won't raise a fuss with yourself if you don't put money into savings this week. However, your mortgage company or credit card company will strongly object if you miss a payment. They will scream and threaten you if you don't make your monthly payment. (In fact, if you ever feel lonely, just skip a mortgage payment. Your bank will give you some immediate attention. However, you probably will wish you didn't have this type of attention.)

Because of the incredible importance of saving and investing our money, and because we are quick to take care of everyone else's complaints before serving ourselves, we *must* pay ourselves first. A classic amount is 10 percent of your paycheck. In his book *The Automatic Millionaire*, author David Bach suggests that the best way to do this is to have 10 percent of your income automatically deducted from your pay and immediately transferred into a savings or investment account. What is amazing about this process is that in a short time you won't even notice the difference in income. You will be amazed that somehow, you manage to live comfortably on 90 percent of your money!

2. Live Beneath Your Means

Basically, you need to spend less than you earn. If you earn $1 million this year, but spend $2 million, you are broke. In our society, a lot of emphasis is placed on making money and having the status symbols to show our success. This is where the phrase "Keeping up with the Joneses" comes from; the iconic imaginary Jones family living next door has just bought a new car ... well, you can't allow them to show you up, so you must also buy a new car. Or install a new pool, put an addition onto the house, purchase an RV, etc. A bumper sticker once defined the idea of "status" quite brilliantly by saying that it meant "buying things you don't need with money you don't have to impress people you don't like."

"Canadians are embracing debt with unbridled enthusiasm. The debt-to-personal-disposable-income ratio is now at 117 percent, versus 96 percent just five years ago."[1] You can almost hear the jail door of financial bondage clanging shut behind the average Canadians who continue to buy new furniture, electronics, clothing and other items on their credit cards. One of the fundamental principles of becoming wealthy and staying there is this: DO NOT spend everything you earn. You must set some of your earnings aside for savings and investments. Every time you get a raise, you should keep the same ratios. If you've decided that you're going to save and invest at least 10 percent of your income, then if you get a bonus or a raise, you should save at least the same 10 percent on those incomes.

3. Don't Pay for Expenses on Credit—Pay Cash

Our money belief system will affect our purchasing decisions. Some people will look at a new television set and think, "Well, I don't have the money, but I've been working really hard lately

1 www.creditcanada.com

so I feel that I deserve a new TV." And, because they don't have the cash, they purchase the item on credit.

Here is a good criterion to determine if you should buy something. It's really quite simple: you should only buy an expense item (something that doesn't help to generate money) if you actually have the cash to pay for it. But many people use the opposite decision-making process. They believe they should purchase that item (electronic equipment, furniture, clothing, etc.) if they feel like it. Wealthy people don't make investment decisions because they feel like it; they make an investment decision because it fits into their long-term strategy for wealth accumulation.

There is a good time that you should go into debt, and that is when the debt is to purchase an asset (something that will generate money). In this case, it is called "good debt." For example, getting a loan to buy an apartment building, a restaurant franchise, or any type of money-generating business are all examples of "good debt." Also, advertising to generate business, tools or equipment for your business, training and education to increase your value and ability to make money are also examples of "good debt."

Don't get sucked into the poor-man's thinking pattern that you deserve something just because you feel like it; think like a wealthy person and make your purchase when you've got the cash in your pocket. Increase your financial discipline. Perhaps you can set a savings goal and build a reward into it. For example, when you save $10,000, you take the next $1,000 and treat yourself to something fun. After all, wealthy people also know how to enjoy life!

4. Buy Assets, not Expenses

Robert Kiyosaki says, "Rich people buy assets. Poor people buy expenses. Middle-class people buy expenses and *think* that they are buying assets." Robert defines an asset as "something that generates money and allows you to eat." He defines a liability as "something that costs money and will eat *you*."

Here is a trick question to consider: "Is your house an asset?" Think about this. The answer is *yes*. Now, here's the second half of the trick question: "Who is your house an asset for?" The answer is *whoever owns the equity*. If you are paying the bank to live in your house, the house is an asset for the bank. If you own the house and are renting it out to tenants, the house is generating money for you, and it is your asset.

The same thing goes for your car. A car depreciates immediately and is a disposable product, like a razor blade. You use it up, drive it into the ground (or until your lease comes up) and get a new car. Cars wear out and don't generate money (unless you rent them out or are a taxi cab or delivery service.)

Now, the bank and insurance company will have us believe that our electronics and jewelry and other material possessions are assets (once we liquidate them and generate cash.) If you are in dire financial straits and you can't sell your diamond necklace, is it an asset? No.

Challenge yourself to re-think your "accumulated wealth." What do you own that generates money, and what do you own that costs money? And then get serious about buying assets that generate money.

5. Don't Work for Money; Make Money Work for You

Employees and self-employed professionals sell their time for money. The challenge with this concept is that you can only sell up 16 to 20 hours a day (assuming you only sleep each day for four to eight hours.) The next important factor is how much money is each hour worth? It's possible to earn several hundred thousand dollars a year as a successful professional or a commissioned salesperson. Salespeople get paid for each sale they make, and their skill and work ethic contribute to their sales success. In contrast, a salaried employee gets to work as many hours as needed ("Sorry Bob; I need you to stay late tonight and finish that assignment.") but get paid the same amount no matter how late they work. If a salaried employee gets paid for 40 hours and works 50, he or she gets paid for 40 hours.

To accumulate wealth, you must make sure your money—or other people's money—is working for you. Rich people who stay rich almost always own businesses, real estate or investments. A business that you own can generate money for you night and day. Think about the classic example of a fast-food restaurant: a group of high-school students are flipping burgers, taking orders and collecting cash. A successful fast-food franchise generates money for the owner, whether the owner is physically in the building, off in a different city launching yet another franchise, or floating on their yacht in the Mediterranean. You must earn money while you sleep. This is called residual income. You can also earn residual income through rental property, book and music sales, dividends on investments, intellectual property, the sale of any product or invention, and so forth. J. Paul Getty is reputed to have remarked, "I would prefer to earn 1 percent of 100 people's efforts, rather than 100 percent of my own."

6. Strategically Reduce Debt

It doesn't matter how much money you make; what matters is how much you keep and how fast it grows. If the wealth you earn is going to paying off high-interest debt (usually from consumer expenses for lifestyle), then the person who seems wealthy on the outside will forever live on a treadmill of making interest payments on his or her debt.

How do you strategically eliminate debt? First of all, don't think of all of your debt payments as separate payments; rather, think of them as one big payment. Add up all of the payments you make each month (not including your mortgage) and determine the amount. Let's say this number equals $1000 a month that you are spending on interest charges for debt. This is your one big payment number. Now, list the debt payments on a piece of paper in order from the highest interest rate to the lowest. Whatever you need to do, eliminate the first item on your list. Work overtime, cut expenses, have a yard sale; whatever it takes. Create emotional momentum towards debt reduction and feel proud for eliminating the first item.

Generally speaking, you should pay off the items with the highest interest rate first. Once you do, the money you have freed up does not go to purchasing a new pair of shoes, but rather you use that money to pay off the next item on the list. For example, if paying off your Visa card frees up $100 a month in interest payments, most people feel that they now only have $900 a month in interest payments to make, and they have an extra $100 that they can spend on shopping! This is not the correct approach. You should still pay one big payment of $1000 a month, but now that $100 a month will be put towards paying off the principal on the next item on the list. This will accelerate the speed at which you pay off the remaining debts.

For many people, the interest that accumulates on their home is staggering. Most people automatically sign up for a 25- or 30-year mortgage, just because their peer group does. By doing so, you are almost doubling the total amount of money that you will pay the bank on your mortgage. If you double the amount of your monthly mortgage payment, you will reduce the length of a 25-year mortgage down to roughly eight years.

Phone your bank immediately and ask for an amortization chart. This is a chart that shows the difference between how much interest you are paying, versus how much principal you are paying down. As the years march on, the amortization schedule allows more and more of the money you pay each month to be applied to the actual principal portion of the debt you owe on your mortgage. But for the majority of homeowners, after years of making mortgage payments they have succeeded in only paying for the front door of their home!

Paying down your mortgage is usually the last debt to reduce, because the interest rate is usually lower than most other debts and the principal is usually high. So, what can you do to reduce your mortgage? First, increase your monthly payment to the maximum amount allowed. A simple way of starting to do this is by making bi-weekly or weekly payments instead of monthly; thus you are making 26 payments a year, instead of 24 (12 months). Next, set up a meeting with your banker to increase you maximum allowable amount, so that you do not suffer a pre-payment penalty. You should consider taking your business to another bank if it won't increase your maximum allowable amount. And you might consider using your home to generate income by renting out a room or a basement apartment. Give someone else a comfortable place to live and get on his feet financially, and he can help you pay off your mortgage in the process!

7. Make Compound Interest Work for You

The power of compound interest is staggering. You can amass a fortune over the long term if you don't procrastinate. For example, consider a story of twin brothers who are investing for their retirement. Starting at the age of 20, the first brother puts aside $100 a month or $1200 a year till the age of 30 at a 10 percent growth rate. The first brother stops investing at 30 and never puts another penny of his money into the investment fund. After 10 years he has a $12,000 base in investments that grow on a compound basis by 10 percent each year.

Now, the second brother starts investing $100 a month at the age of 30. He continues to put $100 a month into a retirement fund that adds 10 percent compound interest each year. The second brother will never catch up to the first brother.

Compound interest is a powerful ally when it is working for you and a terrible enemy when it is working against you. It can dig you into a hole that takes years to get out of. Many people choose to only pay the minimum payment each month on their credit cards. With accumulating interest working against them, it will take them decades to pay off their credit card balances. Make compound interest your ally by investing and watching your nest egg grow.

The Stone Mason

Hundreds of years ago, a stone mason was contracted by the King of the day to carve the ornate entrance to a beautiful cathedral. The King, recognizing the talent of the stone mason and being a generous man, made him an offer: he would pay the stone mason the equivalent of $100,000 in that day's money. The stone mason thanked the King for his generous offer and countered with one of his own.

"Your Majesty," said the mason. "I know what I am worth, and how much time and energy a project of this size will require of me. I don't feel that my effort is worth $100,000. However, I'd like to make you a different offer. I understand you are an enthusiast about the game of chess?" The King nodded. "Well, then, let's do this. The chessboard has 64 squares in total. I would like you to pay me a penny on the first day and simply double that amount each day for 64 days. On my first day of work, I propose you pay me a single grain of wheat (which would equal one penny), and place that grain of wheat on the chessboard. The next day of work, simply double that to two grains of wheat. The third day, simply double it again to four grains of wheat, and so on. I estimate it will take me just over two months to complete the task; if I need more than 64 days, I will work the remaining days for free. Do you accept my terms?"

Well, the King thought about it. On the one hand, he felt that the mason did deserve $100,000 because he was highly skilled and would do a wonderful job. On the other hand, the mason was requesting a grain of wheat doubled each day. The king reluctantly agreed to the stone mason's terms, feeling the mason would not be paid what he was worth.

What would you do? If you had the opportunity to be paid a flat rate of $100,000 for even one month of work, or you could decide to be paid 1 cent a day, which would you choose? For most people, $100k might sound amazing. Think of what you could do with it! You could pay off any consumer debt, mortgage or educational loans you might have; you could help your family; you could give some money to charity; you could sock the money away for long-term investment growth—or you could go shopping! A home theater, a new sports car or luxury sedan, several amazing vacations, a nice motor home … the possibilities are almost endless! For many people, it would be like winning a small lottery.

Did you choose the penny a day, doubled each day? If you did, you are a shrewd wealth builder. You see, the first day, you would get 1 cent; the second day, 2 cents; the third day, 4 cents; by the tenth day, you've earned $5.12! It would take until the 25th day to finally catch up and pass $100,000, but you've got six days left. On the 30th day, you'd earn over $5.3 million and, on the 31st day, you'd earn over $10.7 million dollars! (Try this exercise and test these numbers with a calculator to confirm for yourself how quickly money can compound.) How did the stone mason fare after 64 days? By the final day of work, the king owed him over

$92,233 trillion, and was forced to give the entire kingdom over to the stone mason in order to pay the debt!

(Worthy of note: this is based on an old story that seems to start with the inventor of the game of chess. When the game of chess was invented by Sissah ibn Dahir, his king, Shirhram, was so happy that he granted Sissah any reward that he desired. It was said that Sissah requested one grain of wheat for the first square on the chess board, two grains for the second square, four grains for the third square, eight grains for the fourth square and so on; each square being double the amount on the previous square.)

Einstein referred to compound interest as "the eighth wonder of the world." Compound interest is an extremely powerful tool, especially when we are using it to our advantage and building our own wealth. But most people have compound interest working against them in the form of high-interest debt payments. In this very common scenario, the crushing weight of compound interest becomes an inescapable trap of quicksand. If you can learn to use the concept of compounding to your advantage, you will have harnessed one of the most powerful tools of wealth creation.

What Are Your Money Beliefs?

Robert Kiyosaki, author of *Rich Dad Poor Dad*,[2] grew up with two fathers: his biological father, who was a superintendent of education in Hawaii, and his best friend Mike's dad, a businessman who would grow to become the "Donald Trump of Hawaii." When he was a child, both Dads seemed on the outside to have the same level of success. But as the years went on, Robert began to notice that his Rich Dad and his Poor Dad had different belief systems about money. His educated father said, "Study hard in school so that you can find a good company to work for." His businessman father said, "Study hard and find a

2 Robert Kiyosaki, *Rich Dad, Poor Dad*. Toronto: H.B. Fenn, 2000.

good company to buy." One father would say "rich people are greedy." The other father would say, "Rich people are generous with their money."

Robert began to see that the beliefs that these two men held were literally creating a money blueprint for their financial destiny. He saw that the way they thought about money was actually creating their reality. We might be able to see this in ourselves and the people around us. Just by listening to the words that people say, we have a good clue as to their money beliefs.

Broke Mentality	Wealthy Mentality
I deserve to buy it.	How can I afford it?
Taxes punish the people who produce.	Taxes help the less fortunate.
Study hard and *work* for a good company.	Study hard so you can *buy* a good company.
We don't talk about money at the dinner table.	We *must* talk about money at the dinner table.
Play it safe; don't take risks.	Learn to manage risks.
Our home is our biggest asset.	Our home is a liability.
Pay your bills first.	Pay yourself first and your bills last.
Learn to write a good resume.	Learn to write a good business plan.
If you want money, ask for a raise.	If you want money, create investments.
Only lottery winners get rich.	Lotteries are a tax on people who are bad at math.
Money doesn't grow on trees!	Money grows from good ideas.
There is only so much money to go around.	There is abundant wealth to enjoy.
Rich people take advantage of the poor.	Rich people create products and services.
Money is the root of all evil.	Evil values are the root of all evil.
I want it, so I deserve to buy it!	I've earned the money, so I deserve to buy it.
It's on sale, so it *must* be a good deal!	I never impulse shop.
I love short-term gratification.	I love delayed gratification.
I'll start saving later.	I invest at least 10 percent of my income.

You can tell if someone has a "broke" mentality or a "wealthy" mentality, depending on the way they think and speak. Consider the following examples:

Negative Money Beliefs

What impact do our words have on our ability to make money? Does the way we think about money affect our financial destiny? Absolutely. Our thoughts and beliefs form a money blueprint that describes our ultimate financial future. If you believe on some subconscious level that it is wrong to make a massive income, then you can be assured that you will either consciously or unconsciously sabotage your ability to create wealth. However, if you are passionately interested in becoming rich, and you understand that your mind is either the doorway or the barrier to achieving that goal, then you must first rid your mind of negative money beliefs that are limiting you.

Over the coming days and weeks, pay attention to your words and thoughts surrounding money. Are they positive or negative? What constitutes a negative money belief? We discuss the most common negative money beliefs below. Some will be familiar to you. Pay particular attention to your reaction when someone states these opinions in conversation. Do you find yourself agreeing or disagreeing? Review these ideas and ask yourself, "Is this how I think about money?"

"Money Won't Make You Happy"

This is a sad indictment against the person who is saying it. Usually, people making this statement are using it as a defense to explain away the sad state of affairs in their own pocketbook. Money can't make you happy? Tell that to a young child who needs money for a bone-marrow transplant. Tell it to a student who can't afford to go to university. Tell it to a child who is a prodigy on the piano, but whose family can't afford to pay for piano lessons, let alone a piano. Tell it to the families who have been wiped out in natural disasters like Hurricane Katrina. Tell it to families who have suffered tremendous financial challenges because their spouse died.

The actual problem is that money won't give you a set of values. It won't necessarily make you feel good about yourself and have a healthy self-image. Scores of millionaires suffer from depression. Money won't fix a marriage you've neglected or fend off the illness you suffer from abusing your own body. It won't make you feel proud of yourself if you break your integrity. You have to do all of those things.

Money won't comfort you when you're sick or depressed, but at least you'll arrive at the hospital in a nice car! Money is very good at relieving pressures that create sadness and stress. Money will fix a flat tire, pay the bills in retirement, send your kids to university, pay for better medical care, fund charities that you support, and put food on the table and clothes in the closet. There is no store that bottles and sells happiness, no matter how much you can spend. Money won't buy you happiness, but lack of money certainly adds to misery. Given the choice of lots of money or very little money, it is definitely easier to be happy with money than without.

"Money Is the Root of All Evil"

100% untrue. This is an often misquoted passage from the Bible that actually reads, "The *love* of money is the root of all evil." The root of all evil is evil values, which lead to people who act in an evil way. Only people can be evil; natural disasters possess no morality, even though they bring tremendous suffering. Money is simply a medium of exchange. What you exchange the money for is based upon your values. If you have good values, you will do good things with money (perhaps donating to charity, for example). If you have evil values, you will do evil things (planning and executing large-scale acts of terrorism, for example). Money is required for both.

"I'm Not Materialistic"

If you ever hear anyone say this, you should respond by saying, "I agree. I wouldn't want you to be burdened with too much money; you should give me all of yours." Are you wearing clothing right now? Unless you hand-spun the cloth and sewed your clothing by hand, you're materialistic. Did you eat today? Unless you grew the vegetables and raised the chickens in your backyard (with grain that you harvested yourself), then you are materialistic. Do you live indoors? Unless you chopped trees down with a hand-made axe that you sharpened from rocks that you found, you're materialistic.

Now, the people making the assertion that they aren't materialistic will quickly respond, "Oh, but I don't mean food, clothing and shelter! Those things are *necessities*! I mean I'm not *materialistic!*"

What do people mean when they say "materialistic"? They are referring to items that they personally can't afford. The mansion on the corner that they can't afford? The owner is materialistic. The luxury car passing them on the highway? The owner is materialistic. The luxury clothing on the person beside them in the elevator? That guy is materialistic. The definition of materialism is, "Where my income stops." Anyone who earns $1 more than the non-materialist is materialistic. Everything beyond what these people can afford is "materialistic."

If someone criticizes people for being materialistic, they should first look at themselves. The two-bedroom apartment they live in—why didn't they choose to live in a bachelor apartment?

The two-door hatchback that they drive to work—why don't they just take the bus or ride their bike? The cut of meat they purchase at the supermarket—is there a cut of lower quality at a lower price?

The clothing you wear, the food you eat and the home you live in—is there anyone living on less than you, with a lower standard of living than you? The answer is yes. So, why doesn't the anti-materialistic person accept the lower quality home, clothing or food? For the same reasons that the materialistic person uses for his decisions: he wanted it, so he bought it. Everyone is materialistic, because our bodies have material form and require material sustenance and protection.

"You Shouldn't Rise above Your Upbringing"

This statement suggests it is wrong to make more money than your parents. This is an unconscionable statement, and the parent or family member who ever chides their children for wanting to be more successful than their parents should be ashamed of themselves. Every child should aspire to the highest levels of achievement, personally as well as professionally. We should each strive to become the best human beings we are capable of being. To shrink our capacity because we fear we would be "showing up" our parents is irresponsible.

Imagine a world where the goal was to succeed no further than your parents. There are only two outcomes: the same level of success as your parents, or less. Stay the same or get worse. The next generation can either stay the same or get worse. Eventually, each family, community and country would decline into oblivion. The only responsible option is to stay the same or get better.

"The Only Way to Get Rich Is to Take Advantage of the Poor"
This is absolutely untrue. If you help enough people get what they want, you will get what you want. If you mistreat people and abuse your power over them, or sell them a shoddy product, eventually you will earn a bad name and your business will fail. People don't maintain massive success unless their clients love them and proclaim their virtues to others. You get rich by helping the greatest number of people. It is possible to take advantage of someone in the short term and get away with making some money, but eventually your bad behavior will be found out and you will fail.

"My Friends and Family Won't Like Me"
Well, if you are arrogant, insulting and condescending, they won't like you whether you are wealthy or not. But, let's assume that you are respectful and encouraging of your family and friends to pursue their own success. People who are self-assured are not jealous of other people becoming more successful than they are. If they are worth keeping as friends, they'll celebrate your accomplishments and feel proud of you.

An experiment was conducted where crabs were put into a bucket. The crabs could stretch and just barely reach the edge of bucket and get a good enough grip to pull themselves out of the pail to safety. But each time a crab managed to reach the lip of the pail and begin to lift himself out, the other crabs would grab hold of the escaping crab and pull it back down into the pail. The moral of the story? If you've got friends and family who try to pull you back down into the "pail of mediocrity" each time you are about to succeed, you may want to consider spending less time with them. Spend time with people who are excited for your success and encourage you without any jealousy on their part.

"Spiritual People Don't Care about Money"
Really? Doesn't the pastor or reverend ask for a donation at the end of the service? If the most spiritual person in the church is asking for money, isn't that a rather obvious contradiction of this assertion? You can't tithe without money. You can't help people who need money (or food, clothing or shelter) without money. Talk to someone in your place of worship who is deeply spiritual and massively wealthy. Your conversation may prove illuminating. You may discover that your religion actually celebrates wealth and encourages you to become wealthy.

How to Create Your Money Blueprint

Having read these examples of fairly common negative money blueprints, take a moment and consider what yours might be. Our money beliefs form a blueprint that we follow in order to build the life of our dreams. If our beliefs are negative, then our blueprint will lead us subconsciously towards financial failure. What are your fundamental beliefs about money that have shaped your entire financial destiny?

Perhaps you hoard every penny and never spend any cash on even the smallest indulgence. Were your parents flat broke when you were a child and are you terrified that you might become broke again? Perhaps you earn a massive income, yet feel guilty about it and unconsciously sabotage business deals or accept bad investments to lose money. Did your parents used to lecture you about the evils of the rich? Perhaps you feel uncomfortable with people knowing that you're rich, and try to hide any material sign of it. Did your parents used to sneer at the wealthy couple in town that drove by in their luxury vehicle? How about feeling guilty about making more money than your mother or father? Do you not want to "rise above your upbringing" and you sabotage yourself so that you don't embarrass your mother or father by succeeding to a greater degree?

This is a profoundly important question. Understanding the root of your negative money beliefs can reveal beliefs that have limited your success. Once you find these negative beliefs, you can work to create new beliefs. Feel free to jot your thoughts down in the space below.

Identify Your Money Beliefs

1. What were the defining experiences that shaped your money belief system as a child?
2. What did you hear about money as a child? As an adult?
3. What hard lessons have you learned in life about money?
4. What are your parents' beliefs about money? Did you adopt their beliefs?
5. What are your current beliefs about money?

1. _____
2. _____
3. _____
4. _____
5. _____

Create Positive Money Beliefs

Now, begin the work to replace your negative beliefs with positive, empowering ones. Listen to the words of wealthy people who have the financial situation that you want. In order to have what they have, you must think the way they think. What are their beliefs? Look for positive examples in your life that you can use to re-shape your beliefs. Look for examples of wealthy people being kind, compassionate and charitable. Listen for stories of wealthy people feeling happy and comfortable with their wealth.

Here are some examples to consider:

- "The more money I make, the more I can help the people I love."
- "I've been broke, and I've enjoyed wealth. It is definitely easier to be happy with money!"
- "I am wealthy. Because someone else makes more than me does not negate my success. I have more than others and less than some, but I am wealthy."
- "Rich people help the less fortunate."
- "Rich people honor their parents by becoming *more* successful than them."
- "If my business crumbles, I can build it all back because my wealth is created because of my creativity, my determination and my work ethic."
- "Wealthy people honor their faith by tithing from a *massive* income."
- "Money can do tremendous good."
- "Materialism is great. By purchasing a luxury car and a mansion, I help the economy and give employment to many people."
- "After achieving great health, a wonderful family life, and helping the people I love, I deserve to have a little fun!"
- "I've worked hard to build my company. I deserve every penny I earn!"

Your Financial Thermostat

Each of us has a "financial thermostat." How do our money beliefs shape our financial destiny on a day-to-day basis? They determine the "temperature settings" on our financial thermostat. Consider how a thermostat works in your home. You set it to a minimum and maximum temperature that is comfortable to you. If the temperature drops below the minimum level you have set, then the thermostat triggers the heating system in your home to raise the temperature back to the comfortable level you've set. However, if the temperature in your home gets too hot and it goes above the maximum temperature you've set, the thermostat will trigger your air conditioning to come on and lower your home temperature to a comfortable level.

How does this apply to our financial destiny? Because our "financial thermostat" has money minimum and maximum settings. If our income or financial situation drops below our comfort range, we will scramble to set things right: we will tighten our belt and budget our expenses, we will work extra hours, take on more business, cancel some purchases that we had planned—we will do whatever we need to do in order to bring our finances back up to a comfortable level. This seems obvious, doesn't it?

Here's the problem. If our finances climb too high, our nervous financial thermostat will also kick in. This time, we will do whatever it takes to lower our financial situation! Why? Ingrained money beliefs. Maybe we feel we're not deserving. That money is trouble.

It has been said that one of the most stressful things that can happen to someone is to win the lottery. All of a sudden, a lottery winner's family thinks that they are a bank. All sorts of fair-weather friends come out of the closet; well-meaning friends and relatives constantly knock at their door for—and with— financial advice. Lottery winners aren't equipped to handle their winnings. They don't see themselves as millionaires, and they will begin to subconsciously sabotage their financial situation in order to return to their comfort level. They will squander the money, invest foolishly, trust people unwisely and be taken advantage of, and basically lose all of their earnings.

But, they'll breathe a sigh of relief that things have returned to normal! They will be glad to be rid of the money, the stress and problems that it has created. Once they've found themselves caught in a bickering war between friends and family about who should share in the money, had some of their life-long friends drop them while saying, "You've changed since you got the money," and been taken advantage of by false friends, the new millionaires will have had enough! Their financial thermostat will do what it is programmed to do—cool off their financial "heat wave."

In order to become wealthy, you must set the "financial thermostat" in your Money Blueprint as high as you desire!

How Association Affects Money Beliefs

Association is as powerful a principle in determining our attitude as it is in determining our financial destiny. You will become like the people you spend the most time with. It is nearly impossible not to adopt the beliefs of the people you associate with most consistently.

If you spend time with people who are obsessed with physical fitness, you will either get involved in becoming fit or possibly drift away from them because you share different interests. If you spend time with people who put down their spouses and have unhealthy marriages, you will (hopefully) not take any marriage advice from them and choose instead to associate with couples who are healthy and loving. If you spend time with people who get involved in petty crime and get into trouble with the law, you will migrate towards that behavior. If you spend time with people who believe in volunteering and serving others, it is likely that you will become interested in volunteering because you've been exposed to it. If you spend time with people who swear profusely, it is more likely that you will find yourself swearing more. If you spend time with people who have a negative attitude or a positive attitude, it is likely that you will adopt their attitude. We become like the people we spend time with.

How does this relate to wealth creation? Simply put, your income and net worth will mirror the people with whom you associate. Ask yourself: "What is my peer group doing financially right now?" You see, we tend to rise to the level of expectations of our peer group. If you are 10 years old, your peer group isn't thinking about buying a home. But by the time most people are in their mid- to late-20s, they start thinking about it. If your peers are self-employed professionals earning six-figure incomes, you will likely feel drawn towards achieving that the same thing. If your peer group just sold their company for $100 million dollars, it will open you mind to the possibility that you too can achieve similar success!

Why would association with wealthy people increase your income? Not only will your beliefs about what is possible to achieve financially increase, but your conversations will focus on new opportunities, developing markets, hot stock tips that are about to yield incredible returns, opportunities for partnering on real-estate developments, etc. This is one of the reasons that wealthy people love to golf! It's not so much the game itself; it gives you the opportunity to network and create deals with other wealthy people in a relaxed and leisurely environment.

Although this is not a hard and fast rule, it has been said that most people's income roughly equals the average of the income of the five people they associate with most often. The point to all of this? If you want to be wealthy, make sure you associate with wealthy people. With that in mind, identity:

- Who are the five people closest and most influential to you?
- What do you estimate they earn annually?
- What are their money beliefs? Do they have a poverty or wealth mentality?

Name	Annual Income	Money Beliefs
1.		
2.		
3.		
4.		
5.		

Action Steps for Wealth

You are now ready to take positive action steps towards wealth creation.

1. Decide to Be Rich

While seemingly obvious, this is the first and most important step in wealth creation. Poor and middle-class people would like to be rich. They would prefer to be rich. They even dream of being rich. But people who get rich and stay rich do so because they are 100 percent committed to being rich.

There is a difference between being committed and simply being involved. When you have bacon and eggs for breakfast, look down at your plate and think about this: the chicken was involved, but the pig was committed! Rich people are willing to take the calculated risk, rather than play it safe and hide from life's rewards. Sometimes, they are even willing to risk it all! But most importantly they focus on their goal of wealth creation, and it guides their decisions.

2. Create a Mental Wealth Blueprint

In his book *Secrets of the Millionaire Mind*, T. Harv Eker describes the mindset of wealthy people. He teaches that in order to get rich and stay rich, you first have to think the same way a rich person does! You have to have the beliefs, money blueprint, habits and decision-making criteria that wealthy people have. Do you see abundance in the world—or scarcity? Do you believe you deserve to be rich—or poor?

Identify and eliminate any negative money beliefs that are polluting your money blueprint. Do you have a mental limit on what you think it is possible to earn? If so, what is the magic number for you? Is there a number that you could reach and cause you to feel, "Now, I'm rich"? Ensure that your financial thermostat is set on high!

3. Think Big

The only limits on what is physically possible are the limits you set for yourself. This is why associating with wealthy people is so important; it changes what you believe is possible. Whatever you believe you can earn on an annual basis, double that number right now and write it down. Stare at the new number and know that if anyone else has done it, so can you. Allow yourself to think about the people who earn that level of income and their money belief systems. If you are thinking about earning $100,000, why not $200,000? If you are thinking about earning $500,000, why not $1 million? Why not $2 million, $5 million, $10 million, or $50 million? These incomes are earned by men and women around the world. Who are these people? Investigate this. What do they do? What companies have they built? Almost invariably, they will likely own businesses or earn staggering incomes as entertainers or athletes.

What net worth would you like to have? Wealthy people

don't talk about income as much as they talk about net worth. Look in any magazine that describes the wealthiest people, and it says "Her net worth is estimated to be $400 million." It doesn't say, "She earns a salary of $50,000 a year."

Lift the ceiling on your own thinking. Read magazines on the lifestyles of the affluent. Visit the restaurants of the affluent, neighborhoods of the wealthy, private schools of the wealthy, jewelry and clothing stores of the wealthy, golf clubs of the wealthy. Envelop your mind in the lifestyle of the wealthy, so that your subconscious believes this lifestyle is normal. Owning a 10,000-square-foot home should be no problem when you earn a seven-figure income; tour neighborhoods with mansions that you will one day own. Do everything to stretch your own view of the possibilities of wealth before you.

4. Set Your Financial Goals
Having raised the bar on your mental beliefs, you must set down your goals. We have discussed the power of goal setting in detail, and the steps required to do it effectively. Here are some questions to consider in creating your goals:

- What annual income would you like to earn?
- What net worth would you like to have?
- Do you have goals for business development that require investment?
- Do you have goals for real estate acquisition?
- How much do you want to save/invest annually?
- Do you have debt you need to pay off?
- What are your goals for your retirement and future security?
- What are your goals for material comfort?
- What are your goals for your children's education?
- What are your goals for leisure, such as vacations, adventures, etc.?

- Do you have goals for helping other friends or family members achieve some of their dreams and desires?
- Do you have charity goals? To whom would you give, and how much?
- Do you have goals for your personal enjoyment such as toys, lifestyle and fun?

Using these questions to spur your creativity and the principles of effective goal setting which we have discussed, begin brainstorming goals in every area of your life. Assign a dollar amount and date for accomplishment for each goal. You may consider dividing the goals into short-term, mid-term and long-term timeframes for their accomplishment.

Short-Term (90 days)	Mid-Term (3-36 months)	Long-Term (3-20+ years)

5. Visualize Yourself Achieving Your Goals

You must firmly believe that you can and will accomplish your goals. Whatever amount of financial success you desire, you must activate the powers of your subconscious mind to attract opportunity and confidence in order to reach your goals.

Your mind is an incredibly powerful tool, and your subconscious can't take a joke: if you believe that you are already in possession of wealth, your mind will conspire to move you in the direction of accomplishing your financial goal. It can be very powerful to write out a positive affirmation statement that fully describes your achievement. In his book *Think and Grow Rich*, author Napoleon Hill says, "Read your written statement aloud, twice daily, once just before retiring at night, and once after arising in the morning. As you read, see and feel and believe yourself already in the possession of the money." Some successful entrepreneurs dictate a description of their moment of victory onto an audio cassette or CD, and play it over and over in the car while they drive. Their message is a vivid description of their victory and it engages all of their senses, describing the sights, sounds, smells, textures and exact details of victory. Gold-medal winning Olympic athletes are renowned for visualizing themselves crossing the finish line first and replaying this movie over and over in their minds until they absolutely believe that it is real.

6. Brainstorm Ways to Create More Wealth

How will you hit your financial goals? Many people who are poor or middle class base their goals on their plan. Wealthy people base their plan upon their goals. This is an important distinction. Set your goals first and develop your plans from there. Once you've decided what you want your net worth and annual income to be, ask, "How can I create this money?" You must get creative. Forming a mastermind team of people dedicated to building wealth is another powerful example of the value of relationships. Hold a brainstorming session with your mastermind group and pose the following questions:

a. What would have to happen for me to increase my income tenfold? What do I have to do to generate my annual revenue in one month?

b.   How can I double my net worth?

c.   How can I expand my thinking? What mental limits do I still have?

d.   What is a goal that is so big that it literally scares me to consider it? Is it absolutely outside of my personal belief of achievement?

e.   How can my product or service give even more benefit than it already does? How can I increase my value to people? What more could I add to it?

f.   How can I duplicate myself? In order for my business to expand, how can I franchise my idea/ skills/ product to reach more people simultaneously?

g.   What problems do people have that I can solve? How can I solve them for the most number of people?

h.   What emerging markets have I not noticed?

i.   Who can I partner with to combine our energies?

j.   What groups or organizations could I sell a massive amount of my product or service to in one sale?

k.   How can I market my product or service more effectively?

l.   How can I brand myself as the first choice in the consumer's mind with my product or service?

m.   How can I attract and retain more high-paying customers?

n.   Who are my competitors and what are they doing better than I? How can I offer more than they offer by a factor of two, five, ten times?

o.   In order to take myself and my business to the next level, what needs to change? What do I need to stop doing? What do I need to learn? Who do I need to become? What relationships do I need to form? Who do I need to work with or hire?

p.   In order that I may say yes to the best business, what good business do I need to say *no* to?

q.   What haven't I thought of?

7. *Create a Plan of Action*

Although we have already covered the fundamental principles for creating a plan of action in Goal Setting, it still bears mention to include this final step in progressing towards your financial goals. All of the passion in the world will not make up for the diffusion of focus that comes from a lack of prioritization, or the setbacks that you will face if you don't ask yourself what potential challenges you might face. You must organize your thoughts onto paper, setting the main goal and working backwards by breaking the goal into bite-sized milestones for achievement.

Summary

Don't you deserve a life of massive abundance, not only in health and relationships, but in every area—including wealth? Don't you deserve a life of financial abundance as well? There are trillions of dollars passing hands electronically every day. These dollars are looking for a home; why don't you volunteer your bank account? You are no less deserving than the next millionaire-in-training.

There comes a point when you've looked at the numbers long enough. You've double-checked your backup plan long enough. You've been paralyzed with fear long enough. It is time to apply the tools you have just learned in the chapter on Emotional Mastery to the area of Financial Mastery. It is time to focus on positive outcomes, to fill your heart with courage and overcome procrastination through bold initiative. You cannot wait for all of the lights to turn green on your journey. You cannot wait for the constellations to align in your favor—you cannot wait another moment! Once you have given your plan the due diligence it deserves, the time has come to give your destiny the positive action it deserves. Anthony Robbins says that to defeat procrastination we must "Take massive, immediate action!" Go out into the world and create the wealth you so richly deserve.

Action Steps

1. *Decide to be Rich*
   Become 100 percent committed to creating wealth.
2. *Create a Mental Wealth Blueprint*
   Identify and eliminate the negative money beliefs that may have been holding you back.
3. *Thing Big*
   Stretch your thinking; what goal is so big that it scares you to even contemplate it?
4. *Set Your Financial Goals*
   Develop short-, mid-, and long-term goals using the principles of goal setting to do so.
5. *Visualize Yourself Achieving Your Goals*
   Fully engage the power of your subconscious mind to aid you in the achievement of you goal.
6. *Brainstorm Ways to Create More Wealth*
   Your mind will find solutions to whatever question you pose; develop a Mastermind Wealth Creation Team, and find creative solutions.
7. *Create a Plan of Action*
   Follow the principles outlined and set up action steps, timetables and milestones to accomplish your goals.

5
discovering life balance

All things in moderation.
—Ancient Greak Maxim

Without question, there are life accomplishments that are highly rewarding to you. There are victories you have claimed, awards you have won, and summits you have conquered. Exceptional men and women distinguish themselves through a legacy of the highest performance in certain arenas, and these talents help shape their personal identity. Perhaps you are an exceptional spouse. Maybe you are the top-ranked consultant in your field. Maybe you receive accolades for your volunteer work with children. Perhaps you are a devoted caregiver to your ailing father who lives with you.

We each have a particular genius, something that separates us from others and highlights our unique abilities. But the well-oiled machine of your life is the sum of its parts, and to fully engage one part of yourself while allowing another area to fall into neglect will have the same effect in your personal life as it would have upon the engine of any vehicle: neglecting one area will eventually lead to disaster in every area. To excel in work at the expense of your relationships, health and happiness leads to ruin. True, sustainable success will permeate every area of your life—or eventually none at all.

Why Don't People Have Balance?

In *The Power of Full Engagement,* authors Jim Loehr and Tony Schwartz write, "Professional athletes typically spend about 90 percent of their time *training,* in order to *perform* 10 percent of the time."[1] We know that athletes compete very intensely for part of the year, and then they take several months off to renew themselves. Compare their efforts to the schedule of the average North American worker. What do we do? We work hard each day for eight to more than 12 hours, do home maintenance and shopping on the weekend, with Friday and Saturday night off for good behavior, and take two or three weeks of vacation a year. The ratio of time spent for intense high-performance, followed by time to rest and recover, is not the same for non-athletes. And because we do not follow the pattern of the top performers, we don't attain their results.

Why don't people have more balance in their lives? It could be for several reasons. **The main reason is that for most people balance simply isn't a priority.** We figure that, while it may be important to do certain things (like exercise), there are more pressing emergencies to deal with on a daily basis. And most people make most of their time management decisions based upon one simple criterion: "Do I have to do this now, or can I get away with putting it off until later?"

If we can put something off, many times we will elect to do just that. You see, we don't have to exercise today. Almost certainly nothing bad will happen. But if we repeat that decision for the next 20 years, what will happen? Perhaps we'll develop ill health that leads to a premature death. Almost certainly we can cancel a date with our spouse, or miss our children's soccer

1 Jim Loehr & Tony Schwartz. *The Power of Full Engagement.* New York: Free Press/ Simon & Shuster, 2003, p. 8.

game, if an emergency occurs. But if the emergency becomes the rule, not the exception, our relationships will atrophy.

We may not realize the connection between failure in one area and failure in another. We may not see how losing our health or marriage, which are common but not the only examples, may affect our job performance. "I don't care if my wife leaves me," thinks the hard-working executive. "Her loss." Then the stress of divorce overwhelms him, the sudden realization that he has failed mightily in one area, and the cold emptiness inside him begins to sap his focus on the job. He may begin to lose confidence, as the divorce highlights all of his personal weaknesses. Constant and bitter conflict with his ex-wife robs him of energy, and his performance suffers.

We may have a Superman complex, thinking that our energy reserves are limitless and that we will never burn out. "I've always been a high-energy woman," thinks one high achiever. "I'm the Super-Mom of legend, driving the kids to soccer, managing my home as a single parent, blazing a trail up the corporate ladder while fighting gender inequities. Sure, I skip lunch, eat junk food and only get a few hours sleep, but that comes with the territory. I'm tough as nails, and I've got more fire in me than the competition. I've always been strong; I'll always be strong." But this woman has blinded herself to the reality that her energy is not infinite, that our bodies and minds do wear out, and eventually we pay a price for abusing our health.

We may suffer from procrastination or even delude ourselves into thinking that we will get around to solving the problem of neglecting our priorities when it is convenient. We may even play the ostrich and bury our head in the sand, hoping our problems will simply go away if we ignore them long enough. Eventually, the problem does go away—but not in the way we would want. Eventually, the problems in our marriage go away, because our marriage fails; the problems with our kids go away, because our children become estranged to us; the problems with our health go away, because our health begins to fail and we lose all enjoyment of life. The day comes for all of us when we have been freed from the burden of every problem we face—and robbed of the gift of enjoying another day's blessings and successes.

Why Make Balance a Priority?

If we don't take care of ourselves, we cannot take care of anything or anyone else. Our ability to perform in any area, whether work, marriage, parenting or anything else rises and falls on our ability to care first for our own health and well-being. There is a difference between working hard and working smart. The people who win in life have long discovered that stopping to recharge their batteries is not a sign of weakness, but a sign of long-term sustainable achievement. Consider the following parable, inspired by Steven Covey's Habit #7 in his best seller, *7 Habits of Highly Effective People*:

> A young lumberjack, who was renowned as being the newest superstar in the industry, went to work at the most successful lumber mill in North America. At this mill, the most famed and experienced lumberjack worked. The experienced lumberjack was reputed to cut down 10 trees a day. The experienced lumberjack greeted the young lumberjack and said "Welcome aboard ... I've heard nothing but positive comments about you! We're so glad to have you here!"
>
> Well, on his first day on the job, the young lumberjack gave everything he could ... he chopped and chopped ... and by the end of the day, he had chopped down 12 trees! Well, the experienced lumberjack smiled to himself and said, "Fantastic job!

I've only chopped down 10 trees today … you've done even better than me! Congratulations … we'll see you tomorrow."

The next day came, and the young lumberjack was hard at work again. He chopped and chopped, just as hard as he did the day before … he chopped all day, and by the final hour he had chopped down … TEN trees! Ten?!? Hmmm…. "That seems strange," he thought. "Perhaps I didn't try hard enough," he said to himself. "I know… I should have skipped lunch. THAT was my mistake. Tomorrow, I'll skip my breaks, I'll skip lunch, and I'll be right back on track!"

So, he did that. He skipped his breaks, he skipped lunch … he chopped and he chopped … and by the end of the day, he had chopped down EIGHT trees! EIGHT?!?! Now, a little bit of doubt was setting it. "Why is my performance slipping?" he asked himself with uncertainty. "I've worked just as hard; I skipped my breaks and my lunch … I KNOW! Tomorrow, I'll come in a few hours early, skip my breaks and lunch, and stay a few hours late … THAT will get me back on track!"

So, he does that. He comes in early, skips his breaks and lunch, and works late into the night, chopping and chopping… his friends and family say, "Hey, we've got a family barbeque! We're having dinner, why don't you come over?" "No," he replied, "I'm working late." And he chopped and he chopped … and he chopped down SIX trees …

Then, the next day, FIVE trees …

And, the next day, FOUR trees …

And broken-hearted and bruised, he limped into the mess hall at the end of the night. Feeling defeated, he slumped down into the chair beside the experienced lumberjack, who was finishing his dinner … having once again chopped down TEN trees. And, with tears in his eyes, the young lumberjack moaned, "I just don't understand it!

Every day, I've given everything I've got! Why is my performance slipping?"

And then, he noticed something that the experienced lumberjack was doing, that he hadn't noticed before ... "Excuse
me," he said, "but, what is THAT that you are doing?" And
the experienced lumberjack smiled, and said, "You know, I've
been waiting ALL WEEK for you to ask me that. Every day, I've
watched you work harder and harder ... coming early, skipping lunch, staying late into the night ... every day, watching
your performance slip. And every day, while you are working
harder and harder ... I STOP working, for 30 minutes, and I
SHARPEN MY SAW."

It is important to have balance in your life (whatever your
personal definition of balance) because without it, your performance eventually suffers. Taking a bit of time out of your busy
schedule each day or week isn't the sign of laziness or lack of
productivity; it is the sign of a high achiever who applies the
strategies of the top performers in any field.

Identify Your Priorities

Is there anything missing from your life? Do you secretly feel that
some area of your life has been neglected, and do you see that
your neglect will eventually spread like a cancer and consume the
happiness in other areas if left unattended? Have you ever asked
yourself, "Is that all there is? Am I going through the motions, or
living each day to its fullest? Is there a certain level of passion,
fulfillment and purpose that is still missing? What do I know I'm
doing right, and, deep down, what do I know I need to address,
to fix?"

Whatever is missing from life is not the same for every person, because everyone has a different life situation and different

priorities. The question is: What does your ideal life look like? What is your cake that you would like to have and simultaneously eat? What are all of the facets of a wonderful life? How do you define total success? In order to create greater balance in your life, you first need to create your personal definition of balance. The barrier you face for achieving balance may not be the same barrier that another person faces.

Whatever your personal solution to achieving balance is, it won't require you to spend the same amount of time and energy in each area of your life. If you did, you'd give three hours a day to each of your eight priorities, and lose your job in the process! No, this is not the solution. What you need to do is ask, "What does each priority in my life require of me? What does my marriage need? What does my mind, body and soul require of me?" Do you feel you need to give one hour a week to charity? To achieve your personal definition of balance, you must then give it. Twenty minutes a day face-to-face with your son? You must give it. Each Saturday have a date night with your spouse? You must give it. So, the four stages of achieving balance are:

1.   Identify the various priorities in your life.
2.   How much time do you want to give to each priority?
3.   How much time do you give?
4.   Set goals and action steps for each role.

What Are the Priorities in Your Life?

Your life and your priorities are unique. Take a moment and consider how you would describe these priorities and organize them in your mind. Consider the following examples in the list below and define the various areas of your own life. What are your priorities?

- ❏ Work
- ❏ Relationships with:
  - spouse/partner
  - kids
  - friends
  - family
- ❏ Volunteer work
- ❏ Part-time job
- ❏ Managing finances: paying bills, saving, investing, staying organized
- ❏ Home responsibilities: cooking, cleaning, driving kids, shopping, etc.
- ❏ Number of hours of sleep each day ___
- ❏ Spirituality/Faith
- ❏ Health/Exercise
- ❏ Hobbies: sports team, music, dancing, painting, book club, etc.
- ❏ Managing a major change: marriage, divorce, moving, career change, etc.
- ❏ Managing a personal crisis: death of a loved one, loss of health, finance, relationship, etc.
- ❏ Taking care of an aging relative
- ❏ Personal business venture
- ❏ Pursuing and fulfilling your passionate dream
- ❏ Other

Life–Balance Priority Chart

Now, consider the chart below. Once you've identified the different priorities in your life, consider in a 168-hour week how many hours do you currently invest in each area? Many people would say, "My kids are a huge priority to me!" but they spend only five minutes a day in face-to-face interaction with their child. Some people say, "Achieving my life's dream is my biggest priority!"

but they haven't spent one hour working on their dream in the last six months. Get honest with yourself: once you clarify the different areas and priorities of your life, identify how many hours each day/week you want to invest in that priority, and then identify how many hours each day/week you currently invest in that priority area. Is there a difference? If you think you should spend one hour a day or seven hours a week with your child, but you are currently spending only 30 minutes a week, you have just identified a disparity between your "walk" and your "talk."

Area of Priority	No. of Hours You Want	No. of Hours Spent Now	Goals and Action Steps
1.			
2.			
3.			
4.			
5.			
6.			
7.			
8.			

Set Goals for Each Priority Area

Finally, you must ask yourself this question for each area of your life: what does this priority require of me right now? Set the goal to define and execute a specific action step for each priority you've identified. You may have a multitude of priorities for your life; so far, we have touched on achieving the passionate goals for your future and securing your financial destiny. Lacking compelling goals or enduring financial pressures will definitely erode the balance in your life. As well, not enjoying the work you currently do or not taking the time to have some fun will detract from your enjoyment of life. Later in this chapter, we will discuss achieving balance at work and setting time aside for your personal hobbies. Here are some additional priorities you may have in your life.

Spouse or Partner

If the most important person in your life is feeling neglected because of your heavy work schedule or family obligations, perhaps this requires that you have an open conversation about what is happening and discuss what you can do to make up for the heavy schedule. If you are going into a busy time at work, this is the time to tell your spouse, "The next four weeks at work are our busy season, and I'll be working till 10 p.m. each night. How do you feel about it? What can we do to get some quality time together?" Perhaps this requires that you set aside each Saturday night as your "date night" and cancel getting together with your friends (who should be less important than your spouse to you) for the next four weeks. You may call your friends and say, "Guys, it's pretty crazy at work right now … any spare time I've got will be spent with my family. I'll be off the radar for the next few weeks, but I'll call and chat to stay in touch."

Health

Have you ever known someone to justify burning themselves out in the name of high performance? Top performers who deliver a sustained level of activity understand that they can't escape the physiological needs of their body.

You can skip sleep for only so many days before your body makes the decision for you, and you shut down. You wouldn't pour sand into the gas tank of your automobile, but we think nothing of snacking on junk food because we didn't make the time to get anything better to eat. You can only fuel yourself with take-out food and coffee for so long before the effect on your performance begins to show. Recognize that your body is the vehicle that transports your mind, and decide that you won't settle for anything less than a vibrant, dynamic body.

Is there a contradiction in the level of success between your bank account, the title on your business card and the size of your waistline? Does your body reflect the same level of excellence you demand of yourself in your career? Get your blood pressure level and cholesterol levels checked; it's better to learn of any potential health problems because of a blood test, rather than once the effects of neglect have already caused irreparable damage. Have you started to notice the signs that you aren't as fit as you were in your youth? Do you find yourself getting winded climbing the stairs or playing with your children? Heart disease is the leading cause of death in North America. Your heart is the only muscle that cannot be exercised directly; only through cardiovascular exercise like jogging, biking, stair climbing or swimming can you keep your heart and lungs in shape. The question is not whether you need to stay in shape, but whether you will wait until the damage is done before you take action.

Kids

Is your relationship with your kids everything that you know it could be? Our role as parents may be the most difficult, rewarding and important "job" that we ever hold. We have been charged with the responsibility of shaping the character, self-esteem and skills of a human being. Their physical and emotional well-being is completely dependent upon us.

We may believe that working long hours at the office and making money to provide a certain lifestyle or education for our kids is the key to being a success in parenting. But do your kids want a new car for their 16th birthday, or are they longing to have you simply ask, "How are you feeling about school? About friends? About yourself as a person?" Would they rather you parade them in front of your friends as a trophy child, or tell them lovingly how proud you are of them? What do your children think of you? Do they think of you as kind and compassionate, or critical and overbearing? Do you make them feel good about themselves or see where they have faltered? Do your kids dream of nothing more than to spend time with you and create some memories together?

One of the very best questions we can ask our kids (or for that matter anyone we love) is "How do you know that I love you?" Maybe the way they feel loved is that you give them a hug when you come home. Maybe it's the way you kiss them on the forehead and say goodnight. Maybe it's the way that you encourage them in the hobbies they enjoy. Maybe it's how you take the time and talk with them about their feelings when they are confused and upset with their own life struggles. Maybe it's how you simply say, "I love you, no matter what career you choose." Maybe they feel loved by you because of who *you* are, knowing that you are a kind and honest person. Perhaps by telling the truth and treating strangers with kindness, your children see that your love for them is also true. Figure out how your children experience love, and shower them with what they need.

Volunteering

Do you receive a deep sense of satisfaction from helping others? Have you had the opportunity to serve people in a charitable way before? Did you enjoy a rewarding feeling because of it? And if so, is this something that's missing from your life right now?

If you've ever felt your problems were too big to handle, one of the fastest ways that you can gain a sense of perspective is to give back to people who are in need of love and compassion. Giving money is a simple and easy way of making a contribution, but it is usually more rewarding to actually see the positive effects that the money makes. To be able to look into the eyes of the people you have helped, or even to do the work with you own hands, can make you feel more content. Is there a cause or charitable organization that you believe in? Have you been thinking of this for some time and making the excuse that right now you are too busy? Try taking a Saturday afternoon and visiting with the people that do the work you have been considering. Commit to do a few hours of volunteer work on a trial basis, and experiment with a few different charitable causes to see which one feels more rewarding to you.

Faith
Perhaps practicing your faith is part of your family culture, and your ignoring it has driven a wedge between you and your loved ones. If spirituality is important to you, neglecting it may leave a void in your life. You may feel a sense of guilt that you are ignoring your spiritual obligations. Perhaps you've gone through a time of tremendous challenge or change, and pursuing your faith creates a feeling of security and peace. You may have lost your spouse to cancer; your child may have been crippled in a car accident. Perhaps you are struggling with your own addictions. Knowing that someone loves you when the rest of your life seems so challenging may offer the spiritual support that you need to make it through each day.

Family and Friends
Neglected relationships eventually atrophy. If your family and friends invite you to spend time with them, and your consistent

answer is "Sorry, I'm busy," they will eventually get the message: "Stop phoning me. I'm not coming." Keep ignoring your friends, and they will eventually go away.

Most parents simply want their adult children to be appreciative and friendly to them, to respect them for what they have done for them. Most parents sacrifice tremendously for their children, both in time, money, effort and heartache. Is it too much to ask to simply phone them, or write them a letter to say that you love, respect and appreciate the good things they've done for you? Don't let their mistakes cloud your mind. Most parents try to do the best they can; if you are a parent, you've already made some mistakes. Would you hope that your children can one day forgive you for the small errors in your performance as their guardian and mentor?

In some family situations, the hurt runs deeper than simply being irritated with your family at the Thanksgiving dinner table. You may have tremendous tension or heartbreak in your relationship with certain family members. Your parents may have been emotionally unavailable, given you into foster care as a child, or even abused you. It's up to you to decide if you will ever forgive them for the small or large hurts and injustices they have leveled against you. Perhaps you've become estranged from your mother or father because of the way they've treated you. Do you want to wait to get closure with your mother or father on their deathbed? You may miss your chance.

Forgiveness is a tool that is often spoken of, and frequently misunderstood. Forgiveness of the people who have hurt you does not exonerate them from their actions, or make what they did okay. Abuse of any kind is never acceptable. Forgiveness is a tool for you to let go of the anger that is eating a hole through your heart and your health. Being angry at someone for hurting you or wanting revenge on them for their injustices doesn't bring that person to justice. Instead, hating someone and wanting revenge on him or her is like you drinking poison, while wanting the object of your hatred to die. Your anger only hurts you; it doesn't negate what the abuser has done to you. Forgiveness lets *you* off the emotional hook.

Emotional Health

Many people think only of the external signs of success: career advancement, material success, social recognition. But what value is it to have all the money and toys, if you don't have emotional health? If you are manic depressive, overwhelmed with anxiety or crippling phobias, isn't it fair to say that the material success you may have achieved will seem irrelevant to you? The acid test of whether or not you are successful is whether or not you are happy. Fame, fortune and power are meaningless if you wake up disliking yourself or your life. The simple things in life can fill you with the greatest joy: roaring with laughter, experiencing someone else's compassion, feeling proud of yourself, falling in love, the birth of a new child. The wealthiest among us enjoy the priceless treasure of a healthy mind.

Which Balls Are You Juggling?

In conclusion, as you clarify your priorities, set goals and take action on them, always remember the impact that neglecting a critical area of your life will have. Some things are not repairable once the damage is done. Resolve to take action and address any key priority that you feel you've neglected. Consider the following story, and make the decision to treat every area of your life as the priority it is In a university commencement address several years ago, Brian Dyson, then CEO of Coca Cola Enterprises, spoke of the relation of work to one's other commitments:

Imagine life as a game in which you are juggling some five balls in the air. You name them—work, family, health, friends and spirit—and you're keeping all of these in the air. You will soon understand that work is a rubber ball. If you drop it, it will bounce back.

But the other four balls—family, health, friends and spirit are made of glass. If you drop one of these, they will be irrevocably scuffed, marked, nicked, damaged or even shattered. They will never be the same. You must understand that and strive for balance in your life. How? ...

Don't set your goals by what other people deem important. Only you know what is best for you. Don't take for granted the things closest to your heart. Cling to them as you would your life for without them, life is meaningless."

Create Balance at Work

The challenge with most people's concept of balance is that they feel that they will get around to enjoying their life experience "someday"; on that someday, they'll sit back and enjoy the fruits of their labor; someday they will let loose and have some fun; someday they will partake in all of the life experiences that they've been meaning to enjoy.

The majority of people work all week in order to escape Friday night into their weekend, they work 50 weeks a year to escape from their life for two weeks. Scheduling "balance" activities during the evenings and weekends when you still don't like your career is like re-arranging the deck chairs on the Titanic: it gives the illusion of progress with no fundamental impact in the outcome of your situation. In order to have a fully engaged and rewarding life experience, you need to be working at something each day that you enjoy. It doesn't have to be your life's dream, but if you're having a miserable time each day on the job, nothing in the world will give you balance until you correct that line item first.

Having a deeply rewarding life experience is dramatically affected by your enjoyment of your job, career or your own business. Most people work an average of eight to 10 hours a day. Self-employed entrepreneurs sometimes joke that they only have to work half-days: which 12 hours is up to them. Whatever your schedule, if you are awake 16 to 20 hours a day and spend eight to 10 hours earning money, then half of your day is spent at a job. Balance in life is fundamentally affected first and foremost by doing something you enjoy, preferably something that you passionately love.

Your Attitude at Work

At work as in life, there are certain things that you can control, and certain things you can't. Many people expend a tremendous amount of energy and focus on things that they cannot control in their lives: traffic, weather and taxes. While these things may frustrate you, there is very little that you can do to change them at the moment of your frustration. At work, there are many things that can affect your enjoyment of your job: whether or not you find the work fulfilling; whether or not you are fairly paid for your work; whether or not you get along with your colleagues; whether or not the workload is manageable; whether or not your personality meshes with your manager's; whether or not the clients are polite to you. All of these things can affect your enjoyment of your career.

But, you may not necessarily have control over them. If you are a salaried employee, you may have zero control over your pay! If you are in a commissioned sales position and you want to make more money, you can sell more products. But you may not have control over market demand, manufacturing delays, delivery schedules, or even pricing of the product you sell. You may dislike your manager, but are not approved to transfer to another department for another year. You may complain to your spouse about the colleague in the next cubicle who irritates you each day, who refuses to change his or her behavior despite your repeated diplomatic requests. Each one of these things could potentially be changed—but perhaps months or years from now—and probably not today.

There is, however, one thing that you can change instantly that will have dramatic impact upon your enjoyment of the day—your attitude. You have the choice of looking at things in a positive light. You have the choice to find the fun in what you are doing. You can choose to see what is right about your situation, rather than what is wrong. You can feel lucky to have the job you have.

Many thousands of people would trade their daily problems for yours, in a heartbeat. You're feeling frustrated that the photocopier is jammed again? Tell it to a single mom trying to make her rent payment this month, juggling three minimum-wage jobs. You're upset that your manager took the credit for your work again? Tell it to people who are sold into slavery. You're upset that you've been passed up for a promotion? Tell it to people working 18 hours a day in a salt mine, hoping to get a bigger chunk of bread with their soup.

Apply the principles of emotional mastery and positive attitude to your work experience. Ask yourself: "What's great about this? Why am I so lucky that I get to solve this problem?" We are so quick to forget the blessings that we enjoy and focus on the little things that irritate us about where we work.

You've been overloaded with work because of layoffs. You've still got a job! You have to commute two hours one way. You've still got a job! Your paycheck is too small for your lifestyle. You've still got a job!

People who make $30,000 complain that they don't make $40,000. If they could just make more, it would solve all of their problems. People making $100,000 complain that they are not making $150,000. Understand this: someone is dreaming of making the money you are dissatisfied making, of doing what you are dissatisfied doing. Your current life situation is someone else's dream come true.

People often wake up Monday morning and grumble, "Why do I have to get up and go to work?" Motivational speaker Les Brown has this to say: "Every day that I wake up, and I don't have a white chalk outline around my body ... it's a GREAT DAY!" Why don't you choose to be the most energetic, positive, friendly, can-do employee in your office? Why don't you choose to skip through the hallways Monday morning and shout "Happy Monday!" When people ask "How was your weekend?" you can say, "Great, but I had to wait three days to get to come back to work!" And when you get to Friday and people say "T-G-I-F, Thank goodness it's Friday," you can say, "Yeah, thank goodness it's Friday, because it's only three more days until Monday!"

When you get to work, ask, "How can I have fun doing this? How can I make someone else smile? How can I make a difference to someone today? How can I find my work more rewarding?" Ask positive questions, and your mind will respond with positive answers.

Energy Level at Work

We only have control over ourselves. We've discussed how we can control our mind and have a positive attitude to enjoy work. The second thing that we have control over is our bodies.

Have you ever had a day at work where the enemy was your own body? Perhaps you were fighting illness or fatigue. Maybe you were run down with a cold, up all night coughing and sniffling, or tending to your newborn baby. When you go into work on those days, doesn't the day just seem harder? Don't problems just seem bigger in your mind, even though they are not? And, if you can intellectually see the way to fix the problems, don't you struggle on those difficult days to have the energy to do what you know you should do? Absolutely. There is a mind-body connection, and if we are fighting illness or fatigue you are at war with your own body. So what can you do to take positive action?

Put a Higher Quality Fuel in Your Engine

Recognize that your body is a high-performance vehicle that requires the highest quality fuel. Your body runs on two fuels: oxygen and glucose (sugar). Much attention has been given lately to low-carb diets, but the fact is: your body must have sugar to run. If you don't eat properly, you simply won't have energy, and your challenges will seem harder to face.

The common remedy for low sugar can be seen in the early morning lineups and drive-through windows across North America: we wake up, feel sluggish, recognize that we need a sugar and caffeine boost to get the day going, so we have our first cup of coffee. And we put in a couple of spoonfuls of refined sugar. Now, make no mistake: you get an energy boost from the caffeine and sugar. In fact, for about 20 to 30 minutes, you're feeling an energy high. But understand the physiology behind your body's systems: if your blood sugar levels go too high in a short period of time, an alarm goes off in your body, and your body releases insulin to pull the sugar out of your bloodstream and store the energy.

If you don't use that stored energy, it is converted into fat. When the insulin pulls the sugar out of your bloodstream, you will experience what's called a "sugar crash" and feel very sluggish and even more tired than you did before you had the coffee in the first place! And what do you do when this happens? You probably have another coffee with sugar! Or a chocolate bar, a soda pop, any type of refined sugar junk food to create a pick-me-up and re-energize us.

The most common sources of high quality sugar are fruit and complex carbohydrates. Consider the difference: a tablespoon of refined sugar will give you energy for 20 minutes. A banana will give you energy for two hours. Complex carbohydrates (whole-grain muffins, bagels, high quality pasta) take longer to break down, give a slower burn and continue burning for a longer period of time. Simple carbohydrates (white sugar, junk food) burn very quickly and leave your bloodstream depleted of sugar later. So, the next time you are feeling sluggish and want to have a sugar-filled coffee or candy bar, reach instead for fruit or a whole-grain muffin and cool filtered water.

Take a Break

Consider what would happen if you were in the middle of your busy daily schedule and your most important client called and wanted to talk with you for 10 minutes. What would you do? Probably, you would compensate for the interruption; you would stop what you were doing and attend to the urgent higher priority phone call. You can take 10 minutes out of your day to take a break. You freely admit you would do it for your most important client. You've got to first sell yourself on the value of taking a break. Have you ever taken a break and found that when you came back you were refreshed, re-energized and more productive afterwards? You can certainly find examples of this for yourself.

Many people mistakenly believe that it's the sign of the cor-porate warrior never to take a break. They skip breaks and work through lunch like it's a badge of honor that they are abusive of themselves in order to be "totally committed" to the company. But the cost of this behavior is that you are never fully operating at your highest level of energy and productivity as indicated in the passage below.

> When you work long hours, two things happen: *You assume you have more time to get something done, so you slow your*

pace; and you get tired, so you can't work as briskly. For both reasons, you work less effectively and make mistakes, which leads to more long hours. It's not a crime to go home at 5 p.m. [or take a lunch break]; organized people do it all the time. It's a sign of an efficient, productive worker."[2]

Do you ever hit a mid-afternoon slump? Is there a consistent point in the day when you can feel your energy level plummet and you would love nothing more than to take a nap? You need to be aware our own energy levels and fatigue as it occurs naturally while the day drags on. Many people find that a well-timed period of rest in the day is all that it takes to boost their feelings of vitality.

In the absence of any artificial interventions, our energy stores naturally ebb and flow at different times of the day. Somewhere around 3:00 or 4:00 P.M. we reach the lowest phase of both our ultradian and circadian rhythms. [It's been termed] "the breaking point"—the period of the day when most of us feel the highest level of fatigue. The documented vulnerability to accidents is far higher in the mid-afternoon than at any other daytime period…. NASA's Fatigue Counter Measures Program has found that a short nap of just forty minutes improved performance by an average of 34% and alertness by 100%…. While this luxury is not available to most people in business today, *brief periods of rest are critical to sustaining energy over long hours.*"[3]

You don't need to sleep in order to recharge your batteries, although the physiological benefits of sleep are obvious. If you've only got 20 minutes, perhaps you can have a catnap. But you should resolve to recognize when you hit your slump, that there would be intrinsic

2 Alec Mackenzie. *The Time Trap.* New York: AMACOM, 1997, p. 20.
3 Jim Loehr and Tony Schwartz. *The Power of Full Engagement.* New York: Free Press, 2005, pp. 60–61.

value in taking a short break and recharging your batteries with a well-timed and personally rewarding break activity. The major challenge many times to taking a break is not that you don't have time, but that you're not willing to take the time for yourself. You should strongly consider taking breaks through the day. Take the time to brainstorm activities and rituals that would make your mid-day break more fulfilling. Here are some possibilities to get you started:

- ❏ Listen to uplifting music
- ❏ Listen to a CD of your favorite comedian
- ❏ Read a motivational book with a positive message
- ❏ Take a short walk and get some fresh air and sunlight outside
- ❏ Climb the stairs
- ❏ Eat a nutritious snack
- ❏ Engage your mind: solve puzzles or crosswords
- ❏ Take a catnap
- ❏ Chat with a friend
- ❏ Share a joke with a colleague

Live by Your Values

The final area that determines how fully you can enjoy your work is in having our values met through your work. Take the time to truly identify what values are important to you, and what you want to get from your work. As the story of your life unfolds, you may decide to make career decisions based upon fulfilling those values. Perhaps a critical value is being neglected. Perhaps you've been in situations that compromised your values, such as being asked to lie or mistreat people, and you found yourself wanting to make a change.

There is a great need to determine what values you must have at work in order to feel fulfilled. People may set goals for themselves and feel that they are making progress in their career; they may feel that they are rocketing up the corporate ladder. But as we discussed in the goal-setting section, it's more important to figure out *what* goal you want and why you want it. If you don't have clarity on what your core values are, you won't have a strong decision-making process for determining if you should take the promotion offered to you. You may be offered twice as much money, but it means traveling across the country and being away from home Monday to Friday. What's your higher value: the money or family time? You may be given greater responsibilities, but perhaps it means that you lose creative control because your new role involves making concessions with another department. Maybe you are thinking of leaving your job and becoming self-employed—what's more important: security or adventure? Knowing your values and doing work that meets them is a fundamental key towards enjoying what you do for a living. So, what are your values? Consider the following list:

Possible Values for the Workplace
- ❑ Integrity
- ❑ Respect for people
- ❑ Pride in the product
- ❑ Pride in the company
- ❑ Lots of interaction with people
- ❑ Fast pace
- ❑ Relaxed pace
- ❑ Crazy pace
- ❑ High income
- ❑ Maintaining the status quo
- ❑ Creative expression
- ❑ Professional environment
- ❑ Solitary work
- ❑ Analytical work

- ❑ Taking on responsibilities
- ❑ Having control
- ❑ Acceptance of others' decisions
- ❑ Helping people
- ❑ Recognizing a job well done
- ❑ A fun environment
- ❑ Leadership
- ❑ Intellectual challenges
- ❑ Variety
- ❑ Every person for him- or herself
- ❑ Camaraderie among staff
- ❑ Following leaders you respect
- ❑ Ongoing learning
- ❑ Having work/life balance
- ❑ Health benefits
- ❑ Security of a paycheck
- ❑ Excitement/adventure
- ❑ Amount of vacation time
- ❑ 9-to-5 work schedule
- ❑ Working for yourself
- ❑ Solving emergencies
- ❑ Travel
- ❑ Meeting and working with new people
- ❑ Flexible work hours
- ❑ Positive reinforcement
- ❑ Opportunity for advancement

Take the time to identify the characteristics that are the most important to you and then ask yourself: does my current work situation allow me to experience these? What characteristics ask me to violate my core values? What is non-negotiable for me? What is the line that you will *not* step over? And finally, if my current work situation does not allow me to fully experience or express my values, what can I do to change that? Can I get creative in my current position and modify the way I do things in order to more fully experience my highest values? If not, is there a position that I can transfer to within my company that would meet my needs? If not, what career would allow me to experience my highest values on a consistent basis?

Create Leisure Activities

You probably already know what to do in order to achieve balance. You've likely done it before when you've experienced days that were completely rewarding. Ask yourself, "Have I ever had an amazing day? Have I ever had a day that I felt totally engaged, totally fulfilled, completely satisfied and happy with my life?" Most everyone has had some days like that. The key to personal balance is to unlock the code to your personal idea of balance.

Discovering the key to enjoying your day is like learning to bake a cake. Once you've baked the cake successfully for the first time, all you need to do is follow the instructions in the recipe in order to bake the cake correctly again. So the question becomes: "What is my personal recipe for balance?"

Take a moment and consider the moments over the last few years that have been exceptional. What made those moments, hours or days stand out in your mind? You may consider writing some of the names of these days down on a piece of paper, and giving each day a title: "Day at the beach with the family"; "My son's grade 8 graduation ceremony"; "Winning the award for highest sales in my branch"; "Celebrating our marriage anniversary with a romantic weekend"; "Camping with my best friends for the long weekend." What are yours? Hopefully, you only have to look back over the last year or two to think of a couple of moments, hours or days that were deeply rewarding and fulfilling.

Your Personal Balance Formula

Now, in order to determine our personal balance formula, you need to ask yourself, "What are the ingredients of my exceptional day?" The three main ingredients are activities, relationships and emotions. Let's consider each.

Activities

What were you doing on your exceptional days? What activities were you engaged in on the days you recall with fond memories? Were you engaged in your hobbies, work, family time, high-energy sports, relaxation or quiet time? In fact, a great question to ask yourself is, "What are my favorite things to do?" Take a moment and consider what you would do for fun if you had the time. If there weren't any constraints on your schedule and you had a few days off work, how would you fill the time? What are some hobbies that you truly crave doing, but don't currently have enough free time to enjoy? Brainstorm as many possible options as you can. In fact, another great question to ask is, "What was I always doing before I got so busy?" Perhaps you had hobbies in high school or university that you enjoyed tremendously, but it's been years since you've last indulged in these things. What old hobbies have been relegated to collect dust in the back of the attic and could stand to see the sunlight of day? Try to come up with 10 to 30 ideas of fun activities. Some will be very short, only taking a few minutes; some will take a few hours and some will take a few days. Allow yourself to brainstorm freely.

Relationships

The next ingredient in your personal balance formula is relationships. Ask yourself: "Who was I with on this amazing day? What are the key relationships in my life? Who are the people that I love?

Who are the people I miss when I'm away from them, that just thinking about brings warmth to my heart and a smile to my face?" Did you answer your spouse, kids, family, friends, neighbors? Consider each one. Think of how they look, their personality, the blessings and challenges in your relationship, but most certainly the good times you've shared. What does it mean to you to have each of these people in your life? How has your life been enriched by their presence? What would it mean to you if you lost them prematurely, either through illness, or neglect? On the day of your funeral, what would you want each of them to say about you?

Emotions

Finally, the last ingredient in your personal balance formula is "How did I feel on my amazing day?" Recognize that the underlying reason why you enjoy your hobbies and relationships you've just identified is because of how those activities and people make you feel. What emotions do you enjoy experiencing the most? Many people will respond by saying, "I like feeling happy." While that is an admirable general response, it lacks specificity. What is happiness to you? Is it the excitement from the rush of adrenaline in your veins when you leap out of an aircraft at 5,000 feet, plummeting towards the Earth before pulling your ripcord? Or is it the feeling of tranquility when you snuggle into your pajamas and cozy up in your favorite chair, reading a good book and sipping chamomile tea?

This is significant because once you uncover the underlying emotional experience that you crave, you can select more experiences to meet your emotional needs. If you discover that you enjoy adventure, excitement and thrill seeking and describe that emotional experience as being "happy," you may learn that you also enjoy rock climbing and racing Porsche's at 200 mph. On the other hand, people who enjoy the emotions of tranquility, peace, comfort and safety, and describe these emotions as "happiness," may not experience happiness while rock climbing at 2,000 feet. Hanging from their fingertips over a mountain ledge, may not make them feel very balanced at all!

Once you have identified your favorite spectrum of emotions, you can become attuned to new activities that will meet your needs. If you decide that you love excitement and find adventurous activities balancing, you may realize that white water rafting would meet your emotional needs—even if you've never done it before! If you love serenity, going for a walk in the woods may meet your needs, even if you have never been in nature! Just use your imagination, and think of all of the activities, people and emotions you want to experience in your balancing personal time, and you will have a variety of options that will meet your needs.

Daily Rituals

Don't plan on experiencing balance at some nebulous and undefined point in the future; make today a balanced and rewarding day. How? Integrate simple balancing rituals into your daily routine that you find deeply rewarding. Everyone has five or 10 minutes a day to spare. The key to balance is not in escaping to a one-week spa retreat and getting a hot mud bath and hot rock massage, but in enjoying each and every day of your life. You need to create simple daily rituals that are quick and easy and can be done each and every day. These only need to take a few minutes, so that your schedule is not overwhelmed with new items that clog your to-do list.

What could you do? Perhaps you awake in the morning to a CD with your favorite classical music or motivational speaker. Maybe you invest in a massage seat-cover for your automobile, to relax and enjoy the drive to work even more. Perhaps at your morning break, you choose to take 10 minutes and climb the stairwell in your office building or go outside for some fresh air. Lunchtime might see you instituting a 30-minute relaxation ritual involving solitude, progressive muscle relaxation and visualization, all of which will help you feel more rejuvenated.

But the real opportunities usually occur in the evening when schedules are a little more flexible. You likely have home responsibilities, but can you carve out 10 or 20 minutes for yourself? Could you get home and hop on the treadmill, or sit on a recumbent exercise bike in the living room while watching a sitcom for 30 minutes in order to get in some cardio exercise each day? Can you choose to come home and have an after-work unwinding ritual where you kick off your shoes and dance on the living room rug to your favorite music? Maybe you visit with "Dr. Phil" on the television for an hour while enjoying dinner. Perhaps you sink into your reading chair and enjoy a good book with a cup of chamomile tea. Create little 5-, 10- or 20-minute rituals that you can sprinkle throughout each and every day, and you will have mastered the first and most fundamental principle of balance: make *today* enjoyable.

Weekly Diversions

The next type of balancing activities are your weekly hobbies or diversions. These are the activities that might take several hours at a time to enjoy. It's probably not realistic to do them each and every day, but perhaps you can indulge for three hours on Tuesday night or Saturday afternoon.

What are some ideal diversions and hobbies for you? Perhaps it's amateur photography; perhaps you love to travel to the countryside and shoot some images. Maybe you're a member of a sports team and you get together every Wednesday to battle it out on the rink, field or court. Volleyball? Basketball? Hockey? Football? Bowling? Full-contact air hockey?

Maybe you enjoy meeting with your friends every other week for your bi-weekly book club, sharing notes and perspectives about the latest self-improvement book or juicy work of fiction. Maybe you've finally convinced your spouse or partner to take dance lessons with you, and Sunday night you both go out to tango, jive or ballroom dance the night away. Maybe you want to stretch your mind and you've signed up for a weekly night school course at the local college or university on something you simply enjoy learning about: business, philosophy, cooking or music. Maybe you get together with a couple of buddies and pick up your guitars and meet at your drummer's house for some weekend jazz. The diversion is entirely up to you, but often your diversions and hobbies are a clue as to what your passion might be. The dreams you have for your desired life may be hidden in your passionate hobbies. Indulge in them, nurture them and protect the time you spend on them, for they may reveal your future to you.

Annual Experiences

The final type of balancing activity will be your annual experiences. The question to ask yourself is this: "What makes this year of my life fundamentally different from the previous year?" Have you noticed that every year that goes by seems to slip past a little faster than the one before it? The passage of time seems to speed up as we age. And, if you aren't careful, every single year of your life will blend into all of the others in a gray wash of running from one meeting to the next, putting out one fire after another, collapsing into bed exhausted each and every night, without ever having stopped to enjoy the life you've created.

Exceptional people require grandeur in their life experience. We require more of life than the world will hand to us. We must be decisive in our plans for fulfillment and proactive in our approach to squeeze enjoyment out of every last minute given to us. What makes this year special? When you stand at the precipice of a New Year and reflect on what the last 12 months have brought, what memories will stand out in your mind? Create momentous memories that you can carry in the photo album of your mind for the rest of your life. A great life is not measured by how many breaths you take, but how many moments take your breath away.

What are your wildest dreams? What adventures would you indulge in if you had no limits placed on you? What faraway lands have you longed to visit, what escapades do you want to add to your list of conquests, what experiences have you resolved you must try before your time has run out? What is that thing that you must do before you die? If you die without having done this thing that you are thinking of, will you have lived fully? Do you have the courage to write these secret dreams down, to proclaim them on the paper before you with the pen in your hand and risk sharing them with your most trusted ally?

From this moment on, each and every year of your life select a daring adventure or momentous experience to indulge in. Every year, create a few select memories that will live forever in your mind and create them according to the design you have elected for your life's path. Your special experiences will be unique to you; the only criterion is that they are deeply fulfilling. These experiences may take a day, a long weekend, or several weeks. You might decide to create several experiences each year, perhaps even one per quarter.

What will your annual experiences be? They don't necessarily need to cost a lot of money; perhaps you invest a significant amount of time in your charity of choice, or even take a stand and create an event that raises money for your charity. Maybe you take a step forward to promote your own charity. Perhaps you decide to seek solitude and spend several days alone in nature, working on your mission statement, journaling, considering the path of your life and what work you want to create with your remaining years. Maybe you decide that this is the year you finally reach out and mend that broken relationship with a friend or family member, and you create an experience with that wonderful person that the two of you will remember forever as it brought you back together. Maybe you take your family across the country in a motor home, seeing all the tourist sights and learning about the wonderful history in North America. Maybe you invite your extended family from across the nation and the world to come together for a massive family reunion, creating a stronger identity for what it means to be a part of your larger family. Maybe you take your family to Disney World for a fun vacation or go on a Caribbean cruise.

Is there a travel destination you've been meaning to visit? Whenever you think of your ultimate dream vacation, does your mind immediately conjure up an image of one magical place that you long to visit? The time has come for you to take action on living the life you truly desire. Whatever the obstacle that is separating you from that amazing experience, get over it. You don't know if you'll be killed in a car accident next year or die of cancer. You have absolutely no idea when your time is up, or that of your spouse or children; you cannot afford to pretend that the clock isn't ticking. Live your life as if you fully acknowledge that it is finite. Michael Landon said, "Somebody should tell us, right at the start of our lives that we are dying. Then we might live life to the limit, every minute of every day. Do it! I say whatever you want to do, do it now! There are only so many tomorrows."

Go after the adventures in your heart. If money is the challenge, then resolve that five years from now, you will visit that amazing place you dream of. Maybe it's Hawaii, or Australia, or Greece, or Paris … or the country of your ancestors and your grandparents' birthplace. Maybe it is a place of great religious significance to you. Perhaps you can set up a bank account for "dream vacations" and every second week have $50 automatically deducted from you main account. Could you afford $100 a month? If so, you will have $6,000 in five years in your vacation account. Is that enough for your trip? Whatever the amount, five years is going to come and go. You will either be five years older and on your vacation, or five years older and sitting at home—wishing. Make the decision that you are too important to let your dreams slip by. What wonderful experiences will you create this year?

Make Time for Balance

Those of us who do not make time for exercise are eventually obligated to find time for illness.—Earl of Derby

As we've discussed, one of the major barriers to achieving balance is simply not making it a priority. People often complain, "I know I should do something to rest and recharge my batteries, but I just don't have time!" Finding time is usually a matter of clarifying priorities. We may not have all of the time we want for something, but we can usually carve out some time for the most important things. But first, they have to be important to us. So, how do you find time for balance? Consider this example.

One day an expert in time management was speaking to a group of business students and, to drive home a point, he used this illustration. As he stood in front of the group of high-powered overachievers he said, "Okay, time for a quiz."

Then he pulled out a transparent 3-liter wide-mouthed jar and set it on the table in front of him. Then he produced about a dozen fist-sized rocks and carefully placed them, one at a time, into the jar.

When the jar was filled to the top and no more rocks would fit inside, he asked, "Is this jar full?" Everyone in the class said, "Yes." Then he said, "Really?" He reached under the table and pulled out a bucket of gravel. Then he dumped some gravel in and shook the jar causing 20 pieces of gravel to work themselves down into the space between the big rocks. Then he asked the group once more, "Is the jar full?" By this time the class was on to him. "Probably not," one of them answered. "Good!" he replied.

He reached under the table and brought out a bucket of sand. He started dumping the sand in the jar and it went into all of the spaces left between the rocks and the gravel. Once more he asked the question, "Is this jar full?" No!" the class shouted. Once again he said, "Good." Then he grabbed a container of water and began to pour it in until the jar was filled to the brim.

Then he looked at the class and asked, "What is the point of this illustration?" One eager student raised his hand and said, "The point is, no matter how full your schedule is, if you try really hard you can always fit some more things in it!" "No," said the speaker with a wry smile, "that's not the point."

The truth this illustration teaches us is: If you don't put the big rocks in first, you'll never get them in *at all.*"

Summary

Is it the highest ideal of the human experience to define, pursue and achieve your passionate dream? *Absolutely.* Is it possible to do this in a self-destructive way, in a way that erodes your future ability to enjoy the dreams you've achieved? *Yes.* What will it mean to have built your company, yet lose your spouse and children in the process? To have a bulging bank account yet undergo a triple-bypass and be confined to a hospital bed? To have fame and power, yet sit miserably alone in your mansion, not wanting even to get out of bed? Business success without life balance is not true success by any standard.

True success is when you have your financial cake and eat it too, with your family and friends by your side. Life, health, relationships and happiness need our constant attention. They need tending and nurturing, like the most delicate of flowers that must be watered and pruned, given sunlight each day and a protected environment in which to blossom. You are fully capable of living a deeply rewarding life; you need only decide what that life looks like in your mind's eye and design your days and weeks accordingly. Be a good friend to yourself, and allow yourself to enjoy the gift of today.

Action Steps

1. *Identify Your Priorities*

   What are the key areas of your life? Clarify for yourself what you believe is important. Then, get clear about the difference between how much time you want to (or should) spend in each area, and how much time you are actually spending on each. Is there a difference between the two?

2. *Set Goals and Develop Action Steps to Fulfill Any Priority You Have Neglected*

   Deep down, you know if you've been slipping in a certain key area. What does that priority require of you? Take a moment and set a specific goal or action step to nurture the areas of your life that require your attention.

3. *Find Balance at Work*

   What can you do to enjoy your career even more? Can you adopt a more positive attitude? Take better care of your health and energy levels? Ensure that none of your core values are being violated?

4. *Enjoy Leisure Activities*

   Create some personal balancing rituals that are nurturing and personally rewarding. Determine some activities that can be done daily and will require only five to 20 minutes. Develop some weekly activities that might take a few hours to enjoy. Finally, create some annual adventures to make this year exceptional.

5. *Make Time for Balance*

   Remember, that the time for balance will only come when it becomes a priority to you. Decide that balance is a "big rock" in your schedule, and set aside regular time to renew yourself.

6

making a difference

I believe that you and I—and everyone we'll ever meet—has the inborn capacity to be heroic, to take daring, courageous, and noble steps to make life better for others, even when in the short term it seems to be at our own expense.

—Anthony Robbins, *Awaken the Giant Within*[1]

Have you ever achieved a goal and immediately felt let down after your victory? At the mere age of 30, Alexander the Great led armies that controlled the known civilized world. But "when Alexander saw the breadth of his domain, he wept for *there were no more worlds to conquer.*"

Have you ever climbed a proverbial mountain, and upon reaching the summit, felt a letdown? Some of the astronauts who raced into space and landed on the moon actually sank into a deep depression upon returning to Earth; after all, once you've reached outer space, what else is there left to accomplish? Do you know of anyone who has "made it" yet does not feel happy? Is it possible that success may let us down?

There comes a point for all of us when we begin to question the greater meaning of our lives. We may have a philosophical

---

1 Anthony Robbins. *Awaken the Giant Within*. New York: Summit Books/ Free Press/ Simon & Shuster, 1991, p. 489.

or introspective moment where we pause to consider, "What's the meaning of life, anyway? In fact, what is the purpose of my life?" In the end, what will my life matter? Will anyone notice I was here?

Stop reading for a full minute, and think. What do these questions mean to you? Face the thoughts in your own mind, and allow the responses to stir something within you.

You might begin to reflect: "Have I stretched myself to my full potential? What am I doing with what I have? Have I realized the full impact of life, or is there something still left that I should do?" In time, you may begin to realize that while it is admirable to rise from a position of surviving into a position of success, the higher accomplishment is to move from success to significance.

The Search for Meaning

Earlier, we discussed the story of Dr. Viktor Frankl, a survivor of the Nazi concentration camps. His book, *Man's Search for Meaning*, describes his experiences in the camp and the lessons that he took away from that terrible time. In the camp, many prisoners felt that there was no reason to go on, no reason to live. Dr. Frankl felt that there was one opportunity left to the prisoners: to perceive this as the final test of their inner strength, to endure their suffering with dignity, to enjoy the inner victory of maintaining their humanity in mind and spirit, when it had been swept away in the filth and horror of the camp.

Dr. Frankl remembered a statement by Nietzsche: "He who has a 'why' to live for can bear almost any 'how.'" He saw camp prisoners lose all hope, and simply stop moving, their bodies no longer feeling the blows of the guards. Their mind and spirit were gone, and it only remained to have death mercifully come to claim their bodies. But some men could be convinced that *something* was still required of them, some purpose left unfulfilled was waiting for them outside the camp; these men could hold on to hope and stay alive. For one man, it was the idea of seeing his son one more time. For a scientist, it was the thought of completing his work, something that no one else was capable of doing.

In the midst of these thoughts, Dr. Frankl was struck with a vision so clear, so moving, that he felt he had been transported out of the camp: he was standing on stage, speaking before a group of people.[2] He saw himself clean, wearing a freshly pressed suit, clean shaven and speaking with passion. He was telling the story of his experiences, his lessons in the camp, his search for meaning in all of the suffering. He taught the audience that the meaning to life was to discover what life asked of you and to rise to the occasion; by doing so, many ills of the mind could be cured, simply by having a definite purpose. He called this new concept of counseling "logotherapy." And since life asks different things of each person, there is no universal meaning of life; but rather, the meaning of life is unique for each person. We each have our special task to fulfill. Dr. Frankl resolved in that instant that he would do whatever it took to survive the camp, in order to bring its lessons to the world and ensure that this atrocity was never again enacted upon another human being. This act of surviving in order to share his insights would be his contribution to the world. He discovered his mission in that moment, and it filled him with purpose.

Moving from Survival, to Success, to Significance

What is that special thing that only you can do with your life? Maybe you feel that by doing something remarkable, something to serve other people and raise their spirits, their quality of life or even their own future success, that your life will have an even greater impact. To be successful speaks of our personal victory,

---

2 Viktor E. Frankl. *Man's Search for Meaning*. New York: Pocket Books/ Simon & Shuster, 1985, pp. 94-95.

our awards and accolades, our toys and trophies and bank accounts. To be significant speaks of the irreplaceable positive impact you have had in and on the lives of other people.

What could you do to help other people? Is there a cause that you could support with time, energy or money? What lesson of integrity could you pass on to your child, which becomes the legacy for your family for generations to come? What charity could you create that alleviates suffering for families in your community? What could you do to protect children, animals or the environment?

What book or symphony could you write that would outlive your mortal being and lift the spirits of men decades from now? What product could you invent that improves the human condition? What law could you fight for that protects and upholds human rights? What bold and daring act could you engage in that saves a human life? What example of personal courage could you set that would serve as a monument for others to follow? How many lives will be better because you were born? What could you do with your life that would last forever?

With the powers and talents we have, with the immeasurable wealth given to us that we may think, feel, sense and create, we also have the capacity to ask: "What other good can I still do? With all the gifts that I've received without any effort on my own part—whether the gift of good health, loving parents, a daring and brilliant mind, or simply being born free in a nation that allowed me to pursue my highest potential—is it not also right that I lift up another soul to have the same chance at success that I have had? Is there a child requiring love? A family in need of support? A community in need of leadership?"

We are justified in achieving our personal goals. We are justified in enjoying our life experience. We are justified in winning. But once we have achieved personal victory, if we still feel that something is missing, we may consider that we are missing the feeling of purposefulness that comes from serving others. Simply put, success is what you achieved for *you*. Significance is what you achieve for *others*.

We have the capacity to serve others. It could be donating to a charity, leaving a legacy of integrity, parenting our child with love, encouraging others, or even setting an example of courage that inspires men and women to stand up for what is right. What will your contribution be to the world around you? The possibilities are seemingly endless; it only remains for you to decide what path you will take to bring greater meaning to your life.

Donate to Charity

There are many ways to make a difference in community—from your immediate neighborhood to poverty-stricken and disease-stricken villages in underdeveloped countries. Here are just a few ideas, we challenge you to come up with more.

Volunteering

One of the simplest and most obvious ways of making a positive contribution is volunteering some of your time to a worthy cause. The list of charity organizations in need of support is seemingly endless. If you choose to volunteer your time, it's important that you feel passionate about what you are doing and feel the cause has a connection to your core values and personal mission.

The big barrier for many people in volunteering is the seeming lack of time and energy; a lot of their time and energy is eaten up by earning money for their own survival. This is one of the most important reasons why we need to become financially free; we are then not limited by material restrictions of time, energy or money for pursuing good deeds.

What is truly amazing about charitable deeds is that they make us feel an incredible sense of love, and we may realize (perhaps for the first time in our lives) that the word love is not a noun, but a verb—it is an action. You love someone; in other words, you do loving things, and the reward is the good feeling it gives you. The fastest way to remove much of the pain and sorrow you may face in your own life is to turn your focus away from yourself to serving others.

Volunteer with Local Charities

Volunteering does not require that you give up your entire life, career and social network in order to fly off to a remote country for months at a time, doing missionary work. You certainly can do that, but perhaps that level of commitment is not attractive to you. As well, you don't need to make a commitment of volunteering a set amount every week; what about just doing it once in a while? You could help out to set up a charity event. Maybe one Saturday you could spend time stuffing bags of toys for "Tottle for Tots" in anticipation of giving needy children a happier Christmas. Perhaps the best place to start is close to home. Are there organizations in your local community that could use your leadership skills and experience? Here are some popular examples of charities to consider becoming involved with:

- **The United Way** is a charitable organization dedicated to mobilize volunteers and raise funds in order to address local community challenges. United Way volunteers and fundraising efforts directly benefit the local community they belong to. Many corporations have fund-raising initiatives internally; you could choose to become part of the fund-raising board, champion the initiation of a fund-raising effort, or get involved with volunteering time in the community through one of their initiatives in your community.

- **Big Brothers/Big Sisters** is a wonderful organization whose vision is "to provide a mentor for every child who needs or wants one." Many young boys or girls are being raised by a single parent and are lacking a positive male or female role model. The sting of losing a parent to divorce, estrangement, crime or death may leave a terrible void in a child's life and create deep wounds in his or her psyche. By offering your time as a Big Brother or Big Sister, you can be that positive role model and change the direction of a child's life for the better.

- **Junior Achievement** is a fantastic organization that promotes free enterprise and entrepreneurship to middle- and high-school students. Your experience and success in business would be a real-world asset to the students as you mentor them in launching their own business ideas or help them to understand how business works.

- **Boy Scouts and Girl Scouts** (as well as Cubs and Brownies for younger children) is one of the foremost youth programs that focuses on "character development and values-based leadership training."

In addition to these charities, there are likely dozens more in your community that may be of interest to you. Your local hospital is always in need of volunteers to serve at the information kiosk, tending to children and the elderly, or any number of other services. Help is always needed at local food shelters as well as shelters for abused women and children. And there is always a dearth of foster parents needed to provide a safe and loving home environment for children in need.

Decide to spend some time researching the various charity organizations in your community. Look up information on the internet, and potentially even visit with the organization of your choice. By learning more about them, you may get a sense of what feels right for you.

Volunteer Your Professional Services

As well as volunteering with a local organization, your professional expertise may be of incredible assistance in our nation and abroad. Perhaps you are a family doctor or registered nurse; you may choose to go into remote areas of our country and provide medical care. You may be a dentist and could perform corrective dental surgery. A plastic surgeon could mend wounds caused by natural disaster, domestic violence or war. Perhaps you are skilled in the trades or in construction; you might be able to assist with construction or trades work to build or repair homes, schools, hospitals or community buildings. Whatever your profession, there is somewhere that you could donate your talents. Is there a group of people to whom you would feel proud to be connected? Would you offer your services for free, knowing that they could never afford someone of your caliber and expertise? How would it make you feel to be able to help people in that way?

Giving Money

Perhaps the easiest way to contribute is by simply offering money. You may feel that you currently have no time to devote to volunteering, or perhaps you have not seen a charity that inspires your participation. But, you know that there are worthy causes that require funding for research, materials and labor, and you want to do your part. Consider setting up a regular monthly donation to the charity of your choice. Have the money deducted automatically from your account so that you can make the decision once and don't need to remember each month to give. Be sure to keep your receipt; giving money to charity is almost always a tax deduction for you!

You can also give money by purchasing needed items for local charities. It could be food at Thanksgiving, clothing, or even toys for the holidays (Christmas, Hanukah, Ramadan, etc.) that you purchase for children. One charity, Operation: Christmas Child, actually invites people to fill shoe boxes with toys and hand them in for distribution around the world. You are able to select the age and gender of the child you are purchasing the toys for. This is a wonderful charity that ensures that millions of children around the world receive some toys over the holiday season. For many children, it could be the only time in their life that they ever receive a gift like this.

You may belong to a religion that believes in tithing, or giving a certain percentage of your income to the church, mosque, temple or synagogue that you belong to. If you believe in tithing, making that donation can be one way of feeling very positive about your contribution.

PHILANTHROPY

Finally, one of the great blessings of becoming wealthy is that you might be able to give massive sums of money to create good works. Could you donate enough money to help your old high school build a new wing? How about building a new research center at your university? How about a new science lab at your local hospital? Perhaps this could be the crowning achievement of your lifetime, something that continues to contribute long after your life and leaves a legacy of your generosity and vision for the future.

Andrew Carnegie amassed a fortune of over $400 million as a steel magnate. But, it is perhaps his second career that he is more venerated for. His goal at the midway point in his life was to spend the rest of his life giving away his fortune. As a poor immigrant with little formal education, he marveled at how the capitalist system in America had allowed him to work hard and smart, thereby creating his fortune. He went on to write a book called *The Gospel of Wealth*, which clearly outlined his benevolent viewpoint of accumulating wealth. Carnegie didn't believe in giving a hand-out (thereby promoting laziness), but he very much believed in giving a hand up. And so, he went on to donate $55 million in order to create 1,679 libraries in the United States alone. By the time he died, Andrew Carnegie had succeeded in donating over $350 million of his own money to charity.[3]

Other extremely successful people have followed suit and become incredible philanthropists. Ted Turner gave $1 billion dollars to the United Nations, the single largest donation in their history. As well as increasing the graduation rate for high school students, the Bill and Melinda Gates Foundation is dedicated to wiping out diseases that face Third World children, diseases which North American children are inoculated against. And billionaire investor George Soros has created an organization called Open Society Institutes throughout Europe, funneling half a billion dollars a year into education and promoting free enterprise values.[4]

Leave a Legacy

Will you leave something to be handed on to future generations? Is this important to you? Leaving a legacy simply means that the positive benefits of your actions will live past your mortal life and benefit many people, people whom you will never meet. A legacy can be as concrete as an invention such as the light bulb that revolutionizes society, or as formless as setting an example of fairness in dealing with everyone you encounter that inspires a generation of heroes to come. Have you decided that your life's work will survive you? Will your legacy be as grand as building a company that employs tens of thousands of people, or as

3 http://carnegieinstitution.org/carnegiemedal/background.html
4 http://carnegieinstitution.org/carnegiemedal/background.html

intimate as caring for and raising a child? For many of us, the opportunity to raise happy and well-loved kids that will survive us is a wonderful legacy. The possibilities are limited only by your passion and imagination.

Your Personal Example

When I was a young man, I wanted to change the world. I found it was difficult to change the world, so I tried to change my nation. When I found I couldn't change the nation, I began to focus on my town. I couldn't change the town and as an older man, I tried to change my family. Now, as an old man, I realize the only thing I can change is myself, and suddenly I realize that if long ago I had changed myself, I could have made an impact on my family. My family and I could have made an impact on our town. Their impact could have changed the nation and I could indeed have changed the world.
—An anonymous monk, 1100 AD

Be a living example of the excellence you expect from others. People may be inspired by your example and some of them will follow it. Gandhi said, "You must become the change you wish to see in the world." If you want the people in your family and community to behave a certain way or think a certain way, you must become the change you wish to see in them. Have an impeccable code of conduct.

Ask yourself, "If what I was doing right now were going to be printed on the front page of tomorrow's newspaper, would I be doing this? Would I be proud to tell my children that I am doing this?" True integrity is acting in private the same way that you should in public, by adhering to fundamental principles of life success such as honesty, fairness, compassion, industry, gratitude, trustworthiness, faithfulness and a positive mindset, among others. Christians believe that Jesus was a man of perfect

integrity in private and in public. The example that he set is one
that over a billion people on earth aspire to follow today.

Integrity goes to the core; just try playing a board game with
a cheat. If the other player leaves the room, will you look at
his or her cards or move one of the pieces on the board to your
advantage? If a mistake is made in your favor, will you point it
out, knowing that it might cause you to lose the game? People
of high integrity would not think of cheating in a board game. In
the movie *Rob Roy*, Liam Neeson's character says, "Honor is the
gift a man gives himself." If a mistake is made in your favor, give
yourself the gift of honor and point out the mistake. Feel your
heart swell with pride in doing so.

Who cares about integrity in a board game? It's just a board
game, right? *Wrong*. It's a clue about your true nature. But people
who cheat in a card game might also cheat on their taxes. They
might get back too much change from a waitress and not point it
out. They might steal pens and paper from their office and think
nothing of it. They might work in a restaurant and offer free
food to their friends. These people might cheat on their spouse
while away on business, thinking, "Who will ever know?" They
might break their word and back out of a business deal. They
might make business or political decisions based upon crony-
ism or bribery. They might loot the corporate bank account and
abscond with funds for their own gain. They might choose to
dump stocks illegally and cause investors to lose millions on a
bad deal.

They might cheat on a lot of things. Do you still think it's no
big deal to cheat in a card game? Integrity runs to our core, and
so does dishonesty. Dishonesty rots the soul. We can only hide
our true nature for so long before the world finds us out.

In all things, we always have the choice of maintaining our
integrity. We may choose to say *no* to bribes, to insider trading,

to stealing from the company we work for, to cheating on our taxes or cheating on our spouse. We have the chance to adhere to an impeccable code of conduct, so that the words "integrity" and "honesty" become synonymous with our good name.

What influence and credibility will you gain as the years and decades march on, with a legacy of fair play and honesty intertwined in all of our actions? Your towering example of integrity and fair play could become the stuff of legend. Could you hold yourself to such a standard of personal excellence, that when other people feel their personal integrity is wavering, they remember the example you set and ask, "What would this person do?" Some people are starving for a positive example of how to live their lives; they may have no positive role models to look to for counsel. Yours may be the only words of encouragement that those around you hear today.

Make your life a masterpiece, so every person you meet will remember how well you treated them. Your life could echo for generations through the good deeds you do for others, and their personal desire to model the example you set. You may only cross paths with a person once in your life; hold yourself to the highest standards in all of your dealings, and let the life that you live stand forever as an example to follow.

Parenting

One of the most challenging aspects of life, and potentially most rewarding, can be the opportunity to become a parent. In filling this role, we have the opportunity to create a wonderful legacy of love, principles and success in life. It is a life-altering prospect. To bring another life into this world and accept the burden of providing food, clothing and shelter is a great responsibility to take on. But as parents, we are charged with an even greater duty: shaping a human being into a confident, self-assured and self-reliant young person, someone who can successfully move through this world and enjoy the life that he or she creates for him- or herself.

Our job is to protect, provide for and prepare our children for the world they will face as they graduate into adulthood. It is our sincerest hope that they become successful, just as we have that desire for ourselves. In preparing them for life, we work to instill in them the skills and values that will serve them. We want them to be honest, kind, hard-working and friendly. We want them to have happy and successful marriages and perhaps one day start a family of their own. In having children, we pass on a part of ourselves, both our DNA and our personality, and part of us will live on past our mortal lives.

How do our children learn the values and skills that we desire them to adopt? They learn by watching and listening, and the person that they are primarily watching and listening to is their parents. The inescapable fact is that we are constantly setting an example for our children, whether good or bad. If it is a good example, we hope they follow it. Our children watch our every move like a video camera, recording how we respond, whether we hold the door open for old ladies and whether we cheat on our taxes or play by the rules. Some parents mistakenly believe that they can enforce the rule: "Do as I say; not as I do," and expect it to work.

What value is it to tell your children to always be honest, but when the phone rings whisper to them, "If the phone is for me, tell them I'm not here"? What possible lesson do you teach when you tell your kids not to do drugs because it's bad for them, as you are finishing your cigarette? It does no good to explain your actions by saying, "The reason I'm doing this is complicated; an adult would understand. It involves adult values."

Children can tell honesty from duplicity, fairness from cheating and good from evil. Try to stammer out an explanation of why you are being immoral in your actions and watch the expression of disappointment cloud their features. We are the heroes of our children until they learn of our mistakes and moral failures. Eventually, they realize that their parents may not in fact walk on water. Our actions have far more lasting impact than our words. If your actions spring from negative beliefs and values, it will be up to your child to sort out right from wrong—and make the right choice. Children do have a choice.

Twin brothers were born of a violent, alcoholic father. One child becomes an alcoholic himself, turning to petty crime and ending up in jail. His explanation? "With a father like mine, how could I have become anything else?" His twin brother took a different path. He married a wonderful woman and now has two healthy and happy kids; he graduated university, and keeps a secure well-paying job. His explanation? "With a father like mine, how could I have become anything else?"

As parents, we have the opportunity to provide a better life for our children than we had for ourselves. We have the chance to teach them better values than we may have seen in our own home, as we were growing up. We may have had parents who were truly awful, but we can choose to be better parents to our children than they were to us. Maybe you were emotionally neglected by your parents; you have the opportunity to connect with your child and create wonderful memories together. Maybe you were abandoned by your parents. You have the chance to build a secure family life for your kids and protect them through their many ups and downs. Maybe you were emotionally, physically or sexually abused by your parents. You have the chance to break the cycle of abuse, to say that the abuse ends with your generation and will not be passed on to the next.

Maybe you grew up in poverty; you have the chance to turn it all around. Maybe you saw your parents in an empty marriage, or a failed marriage that ended in bitter divorce. You have the chance to show your kids how to stay happily married, to give a strong example of how relationships stay together and stay passionate. Maybe you felt that you had always disappointed your parents and you were crushed with this hurt; you have the chance to fill your children with your encouragement and support, building their self-esteem in the process. Maybe your parents were liars; you can show your children honesty. Maybe your parents were racist; you can show acceptance and teach your children tolerance of other races and religions.

Whatever lesson you want your children to learn, you must become the example of that lesson, and your children will see with their eyes the very lecture you wanted to impart to their ears. In the immortal words of Thoreau, "Your actions thunder so, that I cannot hear what you say to the contrary."

Encouraging Others

The best effect of fine persons is felt after we have left their presence
—Ralph Waldo Emerson

Your example and encouragement need not only extend to your biological children; you can have a profound and lasting effect upon the development of any child (or any person, for that matter). In your childhood, did you have at least one teacher that encouraged you, that celebrated your unique gifts and believed greatly in your abilities? Did that positive encouragement serve to give you the strength and courage that you had lacked before and help prepare you for the world? Hopefully, each one of us has had a remarkable teacher that believed in us and encouraged us. The movies *Stand and Deliver, Coach Carter* and *Dangerous Minds* celebrate the positive impact that a remarkable teacher can have on young minds. Maybe your encouragement came from another family member, another authority figure other than your parents, or even a friend. Think about this person, what she said and did to make you more fully believe in yourself, and think about how her presence in your life has shaped your destiny.

What would it mean to you to be able to do the same for another human being? To be able to set someone on the path to his ultimate destiny by simply offering a kind word of praise? Maybe all you need to do is show another human being that you love and value him. Sometimes we need someone else to believe in us in order to learn to believe in ourselves. Can you believe in someone so much that it alters his ultimate destiny for the good? How would it make you feel to know that you had an impact of that magnitude on a human life? It is an incredibly powerful prospect. Helen Keller, famous for having overcome the tremendous challenges of being deaf and mute through the tireless compassion and assistance of her personal teacher, Anne Sullivan, said of her teacher's positive influence: "I am gripped by the might of the destiny she has laid out for me."

Imagine influencing the pivotal moment in someone's life through your encouragement. What an incredible contribution you would make! What an amazing legacy to leave—your words helping to shape the direction of a human life for the better; your kind encouragement inspiring another person to pursue her dreams with vigor. Let other people's lives be better because they have met you.

Building a Company

Every man or woman who launches, builds and maintains a successful company is making a profound contribution to the lives of their customers and their employees. While many people yearn for the freedom of self-employment or business ownership, few yearn for the tremendous challenges, pressure, headaches and heartaches that accompany the creation of any business—no matter what its size. By simply offering employment to your staff, you are providing a paycheck that will help your staff to enjoy a standard of living and provide for their family's future.

Your customers also benefit. Consider the incalculable benefit that developed civilization has enjoyed from Ford and other automakers; FedEx and other suppliers, Microsoft, General Electric. Great companies can produce a good product for decades, if not a century. Great companies can change society for the better and literally affect millions of lives.

Creating Works of Art

Perhaps your legacy will showcase your creative talents. Our bodies eventually decay, but an idea that reaches a critical mass of sustained popularity can become immortal. Once a book is written, it cannot be unwritten. Once a symphony is composed, clay is sculpted, poetry is put to paper, or a movie is captured with a camera, the work is recorded forever and can outlive our mortal frame. Some people worry about dying, feeling that who they are and what they represent will be lost with their passing. Your mind, your passion, your genius and your creative drive can survive for decades, centuries and, in some cases, thousands of years.

Shakespeare's works have survived centuries and been enjoyed by millions. So, too, has the musical genius of Mozart and Beethoven. The poetry of William Wordsworth, the great speeches of historical leaders like Abraham Lincoln. The biographies and autobiographies of exceptional leaders like Gandhi, Thomas Jefferson and Nelson Mandela. Inventions that create massive positive benefit for millions have far reaching impact. Consider the invention of the airplane by the Wright brothers, the creation of the incandescent light bulb by Thomas Edison, the telephone by Alexander Graham Bell and the Apple personal computer by Steve Jobs and Steve Wozniak. Consider the benefits that people are enjoying from the use of the Internet, or from the operating systems developed by Bill Gates through Microsoft. Scientific achievements and discoveries survive as well. The insights of Isaac Newton and Galileo and the mathematical genius of Albert Einstein have served mankind, not to mention the creation of the printing press by Johannes Gutenberg, arguably the most significant invention in all of human history.

Sometimes we gloss over the impact of our contributions, believing that our creative passion might be irrelevant and fanciful. In May of 1915, Lieutenant Colonel John McCrae, MD of the Canadian Armed Forces, helped bury one of his comrades who had been killed in battle. In an effort to vent his anger and sadness the next day, he sat down amongst the gravestones with his notebook and began dashing down a few lines of verse. McCrae thought nothing of the verses that he wrote and actually threw the poem away. Another officer, upon finding it on the ground, was struck by the bittersweet words he read and sent it to newspapers in England. John McCrae did not realize those 20 minutes of creativity would be a contribution that would last nearly a century and link his name with Remembrance Day forever. That December in 1915, the papers printed McCrae's poem for the first time and it became the most recognized wartime poem ever written. "IN FLANDERS FIELDS the poppies blow; between the crosses row on row ..."[5]

We have incredible power in our creativity to leave a legacy; you may not realize how a moment of imagination can become an incredible contribution for generations to come.

5 http://www.arlingtoncemeterynet/flanders.htm

Turn Sorrow into Triumph

Every man dies ... not every man really lives.
—Mel Gibson, *Braveheart*

Life is not fair; in fact, every human being will face good days and bad, challenging setbacks and wonderful victories, cataclysmic disaster and life-altering blessings. The pendulum of positive experience and negative setbacks will swing to and fro for every one of us. The opportunity lies in what we do with the terrible challenges that we face. We may lose a child to cancer; we may be paralyzed in a car accident; we may have faced terrible abuse as a child. The question remains: what do we do with our experiences?

For many people, the horror that they have faced will define them as a victim, leaving them a lifetime of suffering and misery. But others define themselves as survivors, even as advocates for others who will face similar challenges. Because of their personal suffering, they make it their life's mission to serve others who may not have the strength to carry on otherwise. Here are the stories of four remarkable men and women who have faced tremendous sorrow, and have chosen not only to survive, but to champion the cause of others and lift them as they have lifted themselves.

Christopher Reeve

What I do is based on powers we all have inside us; the ability to endure; the ability to love, to carry on, to make the best of what we have—and you don't have to be a "Superman" to do it.
—Christopher Reeve

While the world knew him for his incredible role as Superman, those who knew him personally remember him to be much more than just an exquisite actor. Christopher Reeve was an extraordinary father, a loving husband, a human rights advocate, an avid adventurer and environmentalist, an author, a director and an accomplished pianist. He was also a pilot who had made two solo trips across the Atlantic, an outdoor enthusiast who skied, sailed, scuba dived, played tennis and canoed alone into the wilderness. In 1985, at the age of 33, Christopher began horseback riding and by 1989 was competing in events, which included cross-country jumping.

On May 27, 1995, a robust and athletic Christopher Reeve was paralyzed from a spinal cord injury so severe that his first lucid thought was that it might be better for everyone if he were to die. Inspired by his wife Dana's unconditional love, Christopher chose to live. After months of grueling rehabilitation and therapy, Christopher returned home. He delved into ways he could use his name, his celebrity and his voice to urge the scientific world to work faster and harder to find a cure for spinal cord injuries; to help the patient community be heard and improve their quality of life; and to impact legislators to increase federal funding for spinal cord injury research.

Christopher defied conventional wisdom. As a result of his courage, determination, international renown and his conviction that nothing is impossible, Christopher ignited a sea of change. Through his leadership, the Christopher Reeve Foundation (CRF) was born and grew exponentially, reshaping the world of spinal repair research. Christopher fought to increase research funding and attention at the federal level by appearing in front of Congress as a patient advocate. And while ardent research continued, Dana Reeve established the Quality of Life Grants Program to aid organizations working to enhance the quality of life for those living through the day-to-day challenges of disability. In order to address individual quality-of-life needs, Christopher and Dana co-founded the Christopher and Dana Reeve Paralysis Resource Center.

Sadly, Christopher passed away on October 10, 2004. At only 52 years old, it was far too soon. The validation of his legacy is that the CRF will continue his journey on behalf of millions of people worldwide living with paralysis, sharing his legacy and banding together in his memory to go forward.[6]

Elizabeth Glaser

The Elizabeth Glaser Pediatric AIDS Foundation was born from the most powerful force of all: a mother's love for her children. Elizabeth Glaser contracted the AIDS virus through a blood transfusion in 1981 while giving birth to her daughter, Ariel. She and her husband, Paul, later learned that Elizabeth had unknowingly passed the virus on to Ariel through breast milk and that their son, Jake, had contracted the virus in utero.

The Glasers discovered, in the course of trying to treat Ariel, that drug companies and health agencies had no idea that HIV/AIDS was prevalent among children. The only drugs on the market were for adults—nothing had been tested or approved for children, which meant that there was no medical treatment for the infection that was quickly destroying Ariel's life.

Ariel lost her battle with AIDS in 1988. Fully aware that Jake's life was also in danger, Elizabeth rose to action. She approached her close friends, Susie Zeegen and Susan DeLaurentis, for help in creating a foundation that would serve to raise money for basic HIV/AIDS research. The foundation had one critical mission: to bring hope to children with AIDS. Few researchers were focusing on issues specific to pediatric HIV/AIDS, there were no drugs available for children, and the

---

6 Adapted from www.christopherreeve.org

infection rate was rapidly rising. Elizabeth, Susie and Susan sought to change that harsh reality.

The foundation's influence has been dramatic. Today, there is an entire community of pediatric AIDS researchers that didn't exist before. Fewer children are being born with HIV, and children with HIV infection are living longer and healthier lives. In every area of the Federal government—from research priorities at the National Institutes of Health to the halls of Congress—children with HIV are no longer forgotten. And while Elizabeth lost her personal battle with AIDS, her son Jake is now a healthy young adult.

What three mothers began around a kitchen table in 1988 is now the leading national nonprofit organization dedicated to creating a future of hope for children and families worldwide by eradicating pediatric AIDS, providing care and treatment for people with HIV/AIDS, and accelerating the discovery of new treatments for other serious and life-threatening pediatric illnesses.[7]

Candace Lightner

In 1979, five-and-a-half-month-old Laura Lamb became one of the world's youngest quadriplegics when Laura and her mother, Cindi, were hit head-on by a repeat drunk driving offender traveling at 120 mph. As a result of the crash, Cindi and her friends waged a war against drunk driving in their home state of Maryland. Less than a year later, on the other side of the country in California, 13-year-old Cari Lightner was killed at the hands of a drunk driver. Two days prior, the offender was released on bail for a hit-and-run drunk driving crash. He already had two drunk driving convictions with a third plea-bargained to "reckless accident." At the time of Cari's death, the drunk driving offender was carrying a valid California driver's license.

---

7 Adapted from www.pedaids.org.

Enraged, Cari's mother, Candace Lightner, and friends gathered at a steak house in Sacramento. They discussed forming a group named "MADD—Mothers Against Drunk Drivers." Thus, MADD was born with a name that would sweep the nation.

In 1980, MADD started with a loosely assembled group of brokenhearted mothers. Today, it is the largest crime victims' assistance organization in the world with more than 3 million members and supporters.

Since MADD's inception, alcohol-related traffic fatalities have declined 43 percent. Statistics indicate that in 1980, 55 percent (28,100) of the nation's 51,091 traffic fatalities were alcohol-related. In 1999, alcohol-related fatalities represented 38 percent (15,794) of the nation's 41,345 traffic fatalities, according to preliminary statistics. Due in large part to MADD's efforts, more than an estimated 138,000 people are alive today and an untold number have received comfort, support and assistance in dealing with the aftermath of a drunk driving crash.

MADD is about committed spirits and determined volunteers. It is the embodiment of victim support and assistance. MADD is tangible proof that social attitudes can be radically changed.

Last year, MADD updated its mission statement to reflect its long-running efforts to prevent underage drinking. The new mission, "to stop drunk driving, support victims of this violent crime and prevent underage drinking," reinforces MADD's commitment to reach out to young people.[8]

---

8 Adapted from www.pedaids.org

John Walsh

A career in fighting crime is one John Walsh never expected. In 1981, Walsh was a partner in a successful hotel management company. He and his wife Revé were living the American dream in southern Florida with their six-year-old son Adam. But then violent crime touched their lives. On July 27, 1981, Adam Walsh was abducted from a suburban shopping mall. For 16 days, a frantic search followed until Adam's remains were discovered more than 100 miles from his home.

The prime suspect in Adam's murder, Ottis Toole, was never charged. He died in prison while serving life for other crimes. Toole took the truth about his possible involvement in Adam's murder to his grave, denying John and Revé an opportunity for closure.

The Walshes turned their grief into action and without a badge or a gun, John Walsh quickly became a nationally recognized leader in the push for victims' rights. In 1987, FOX contacted John about hosting a groundbreaking new reality show designed to track down the country's most notorious and dangerous fugitives by profiling their cases to a national audience. Using *America's Most Wanted* as his vehicle for justice, John could now bring to other victims of violent crime the closure he never found.

Despite his years of exposure to the dark sides of humanity, John still believes in the inherent good of people and their power to make positive changes. John explains, "Everything we have been able to accomplish is because of the public. When I think back to everything we did that some people predicted would never happen—the bills they said would never pass, the National Center for Missing and Exploited Children they said would never come to be—it was the public that made it work. In 1996, when FOX wanted to cancel *America's Most*

Wanted, the public brought it back. I was amazed at the reaction. It was overwhelming, and it was so gratifying."[9]

Courage

The only thing necessary for the triumph of evil is for good men to do nothing.—Edmund Burke

Your act of contribution may not be related to raising money for your personal charity, volunteering at the local charity or encouraging a young child. It may require more of you than devoting your time and energy on a Saturday afternoon, or digging some spare change out of your pocket: your contribution may involve saving the lives of other men and women, sometimes at great personal risk to yourself. Your contribution may be as profound as championing human rights and freedoms, standing up for justice and risking everything to do the right thing. To maintain your personal integrity in the face of mortal peril may be the most courageous act possible to a human being, and the noblest contribution you could ever make. Here are only a few examples in recent history of noble souls who have stood with courage.

Bringing Independence to a Nation

Known as "the Father of India," Mahatma Gandhi is the most celebrated and influential Indian of the last century. He is credited with freeing the nation of India from a century of British rule. However, the greatness within him would not be revealed even to himself until he came face to face with prejudice and was outraged at the injustice of it.

Gandhi began his professional life as a barrister, having studied in London from the age of 19. After finishing his education,

---

9 Adapted from www.amw.com

he took a job in South Africa with an Indian law firm. While traveling across the country by train, he was thrown off the train for refusing to move back to a third-class seat with all of the other colored people, despite the fact that he had purchased a valid first-class ticket.

Seeing the racism and injustice that was leveled against Indians, he decided to take action. He began a seven-year struggle to improve the rights of Indians in South Africa, a struggle which saw thousands of Indians jailed unfairly, beaten or murdered. All the while, Gandhi promoted the concept of non-violent protest: they would not fight back physically even when they were being beaten. The tidal wave of public condemnation towards the injustice of the South African government towards Indians finally forced the government to reach a compromise of peaceful co-existence.

Returning to India, his notoriety preceded him; stepping off the boat, he was hailed as an international hero of the Indian people. His attention soon turned to the challenges that native Indians faced at the hands of their British rulers. The nation of India desired its independence. During a time of great famine, he fought back against the crushing taxes placed on farmers by their British landlords—and won. He promoted the equal treatment of women, and promoted respect among Muslims and Hindus. But it was after hundreds of civilians were massacred by British troops that Gandhi finally decided that British rule over India was fundamentally evil and must be brought to an end.

Gandhi boycotted British-made goods, including clothing, and encouraged Indians to spin their own cloth and wear robes made by their own hands. He encouraged people to stop paying taxes to the British. Most famously, he protested a tax on salt by marching 400 kilometers to the sea in order to make his own salt. Thousands of Indians marched by his side. Finally, as

World War II loomed on the horizon, Gandhi laid down his ultimatum: Indians would not support the British in the war until they achieved their independence.

With mounting civil pressure in the subsequent years, and the terrible drain of the war both in materials and human lives, the British soon conceded to the demands of the Indian nation. After nearly a century of rule and with Gandhi as their strongest and most vocal opponent, the British government finally ceded control of India in 1947. His example inspired leaders such as Nelson Mandela and Martin Luther King, Jr. His complete devotion to human rights and his unwavering stance on non-violent protest became a monument of courage, leadership, vision, compassion and integrity for leaders around the globe.[10]

Leading Slaves to Freedom

Known as "Black Moses," Harriet Tubman was a freedom fighter for African Americans during the American Civil War. Having escaped from slavery herself, she was aided in her flight by Quakers, who had created a string of safe houses among people who were friendly to the abolitionist movement. This was called the Underground Railroad, and Harriet Tubman vowed that she would repay their kindness by returning to free other slaves. Over and over, Harriet would sneak back into the South and personally lead over 300 of slaves to freedom, despite mortal danger to herself if she were captured. Word of her incredible success as a "Conductor" for the Underground Railroad soon spread across the South, to slaves and enemies alike. A massive bounty was placed on her head for her capture, and yet she was never betrayed. Using her wits, cunning and incredible courage, Harriet proudly said that she had "never lost a passenger."[11]

10 http://en.wikipedia.org/wiki/Gandi
11 http://en.wikipedia.org/wiki/Harriet_Tubman

A Defining Act of Courage

In 1955, a black seamstress by the name of Rosa Parks boarded the local bus in her hometown of Montgomery, Alabama, on her way to work. Although slavery had ended in the Southern United States, racism and prejudice were not only rampant, they were enforced by business. Her bus included a section for white passengers at the front, and a section for black passengers at the back. A white man boarding the bus found Rosa sitting in the "white" section, and demanded that she move to the back. Rosa refused. She was tried and convicted of violating a city ordinance.[12]

In one singular, defining moment, Rosa Parks stepped into history, creating a tidal wave of support that was unprecedented. A preacher in a nearby community, Reverend Martin Luther King, Jr., heard of her bold action of rebellion and was inspired. He was a charismatic orator, and his words and his conviction served to unite the black community. He organized a boycott against the bus company, and people stood behind him. Absolutely no one in the black community would ride the bus, until the company agreed that blacks could sit alongside whites. The bus company scoffed at this ultimatum. Consequently, the bus company almost went out of business. It seems they hadn't considered that the majority of their passengers were black. After nearly a year, facing bankruptcy and the ultimate destruction of their business, the Montgomery bus company finally agreed: blacks could sit where they wanted.

Martin Luther King, Jr., would continue on, drawing more and more support, launching a battle of social reform the likes of which had never been seen. He was a brilliant, courageous man. Drawing on the teachings of his hero Gandhi, with strength of conviction and courage, Dr. King led the civil rights movement in the United States. Arguably, he did more for equality in the United States than any person before or since. Using non-violent social reform, passion and

---

12 http://www.achievement.org/autodoc/page/par0pro-1

vision, his legacy culminated on the steps of the Lincoln Memorial, where he told a crowd of 100,000 onlookers "I have a dream!" He successfully redefined the way the black community saw themselves, and the way everyone else saw them.

On October 14, 1964, King became the youngest recipient of the Nobel Peace Prize, which was awarded to him for leading non-violent resistance to end racial prejudice in the United States. His convictions drew the ire of his opponents, and on April 4, 1968, an assassin's bullet would silence the voice of this remarkable human being.[13] But his legacy has lived on. His opponents couldn't silence what he stood for, and his opponents couldn't erase what he had done.

One act of integrity and courage on a bus was the catalyst to change the discriminatory laws against African-Americans. Rosa Parks' actions lit the flame of justice in the heart of Martin Luther King, Jr., and he immortalized her act; otherwise, her courageous act would have slipped into obscurity. But, millions of people know of that pivotal moment on the bus because of the ripples and shockwaves of change that it initiated. One single action or one moment in a person's life could change everything.

Saving a Life

Do you need to save a nation or a community in order to contribute with courage? Of course not. In fact, every day of our lives we have the opportunity to display compassion and courage in our dealings with the people around us. At some moment in our lives, we may be called to dare mightily in order to save the life of another human being. In that moment, we may make the most significant contribution of all. Emergency service workers, firemen and policemen may face this challenge (and enjoy the incredible privilege) any day on the job. Soldiers on the frontlines risk their lives to defend freedom,

---

13 http://en.wikipedia.org/wiki/Martin_luther_king

risk their safety to rescue a wounded comrade or risk everything to defeat the enemy. The firefighters who rushed into the Twin Towers to save what few civilians they could reach in time, risked their own lives. Every day, these brave men and women display exemplary character and courage in protecting human lives.

We could think of classic examples of running into a burning building to save a child, but what about jumping down onto the subway tracks to rescue a woman who has fallen there? What about hearing the cries of someone in an alleyway being mugged, and launching into action to defend the victim? What about administering first aid or CPR to someone who is in dire need? What about helping someone who is choking, or drowning, or in a car crash and needs a tourniquet applied to his or her bloody leg? Every day, people are in need of help. Are we ready and willing to dive into the situation to save a human life? We should be, and we can be. You could be the person who saves another human soul, and that person will feel the depth of your contribution every day of his or her continuing life.

Summary

Life is no "brief candle" to me. It is a sort of splendid torch which I have got hold of for a moment, and I want to make it burn as brightly as possible before handing it on to future generations
—George Bernard Shaw

Sometimes, it is impossible to know what impact our contributions may make upon the lives around us. We may be unable to predict the positive shockwaves that resonate from the slightest gift of consideration, sacrifice or courage. The way we live our lives may help other people in ways we've never dreamed.

In World War II, the soldiers of Western nations rallied together on D-Day and stormed the beaches of Normandy. Loaded down with gear, weapons and ammunition, many of the soldiers had just stepped foot off the landing boats when they were cut down by German machine-gun fire. Their comrades following behind them would sometimes dive overboard into the surf to escape the deadly gunfire, but many of those men drowned in the waters offshore because of the sheer weight of their equipment.

Some of the soldiers caught in the waters managed to keep their wits about them and quickly jettisoned their heavy gear, gasping for air but managing to crawl ashore. They had survived drowning, but these soldiers were faced with a terrible realization: they were now pinned down on the beach behind barricades and debris, and they had dropped their guns in the surf to avoid drowning. Unarmed and shivering, some of them fell prey to the German fire.

But some of these soldiers found themselves lying next to the bodies of their fallen comrades, fellow soldiers who had been cut down by gunfire. These were the soldiers who made it to shore before being shot, and they were still carrying their weapons. And so, they picked up the rifles of the dead men and continued fighting. It was, of course, a terrible tragedy that one soldier died, but it was a great blessing that his death meant in that instant that another soldier was now safely ashore and armed to continue the battle. Those soldiers who died never realized that their death gave a fighting chance to the men in the landing boat behind them to carry on.

The way that we contribute to others may not yet be revealed to us. The kind word of encouragement we offer to a stranger on the street may mean the difference between that person giving up on his or her dreams, or carrying on. The time we stand up for someone being bullied on the street because of their race or religion may change a bystander's viewpoint about prejudice. Telling the story to our children of how we once stood up to a colleague who invited us to commit fraud may be a lesson that they will carry into adulthood. The song we write may soothe another soul. The company we build may provide the money to send our employees' children to university, which in turn secures our employees' retirement. The heroic deed we execute may save a human life. The charity we donate to, volunteer for, or create from our own passion may improve or even save a human life.

When history records your name in the annals of human achievement, what will your life have meant? Does it really matter anyway, if you contribute? After all, there is so much pain and suffering in the world. Even contemplating the enormity of the need, the crushing weight of human suffering that is experienced across the globe, can be a staggering thought. Is there any point in even trying? *Most certainly.* Even the smallest contribution matters, as the following story aptly shows.

A young man was jogging on the beach one morning when he saw an old man ahead of him bending down and picking up starfish and throwing them into the sea one by one. As he came close the young man asked, "What are you doing?" The old man answered, "There was a storm last night and many starfish were washed high up onto the beach. If I don't throw them back, the sun will kill them by noon." The young man laughed and said, "You are a fool, old man. The beach is miles long and there are thousands of starfish stranded on it. You can't get to them all before the sun dries them out and kills them. What you are doing, old man, just doesn't matter." The old man threw another starfish into the safety of the waves and said, "It mattered to that one!"[14]

---

14 Adapted from Loren, Eiseley, *The Star Thrower*. Paraphrased by Rabbi Marc Gellman.

Action Steps

1. *Determine What Cause Might Be Compelling to You.*

   Do you feel a desire to contribute more to the world around you? If so, have you determined what would fulfill that desire? Is there a particular charity or cause that fits with your values and overall mission? Determine this.

2. *Take Action.*

   Call the charities that interest you, research them on the Internet and visit their local organizational meetings. Spend time with other volunteers. Schedule time in your calendar to do this. Donate money. Write a letter to build support. Decide what action you are going to take, and then execute your plan.

3. *Think Big.*

   What larger meaning could your life have? Do you have an "unrealistic" dream of wanting to change the world? Is their a certain pain that you or a loved one has suffered that you want to erase from the Earth? Have you seen injustice, either personally or vicariously, that fills you with a rage great enough to make you want to stamp out the injustice? Has disease or tragedy touched your life? What incredible thing could you do to change the world? Think big. Assemble a group of big thinkers. Every great victory has been born of an idea in the courageous mind of a dreamer. Dare to dream.

conclusion

You have been given a precious gift. This morning, when you awoke, you awoke to a very special day. With each day, we have the choice to either squander the irreplaceable moments offered to us, or squeeze every bit of adventure, discovery, and happiness out of it. It remains only to be seen what you will do with the incredible treasure that is your life.

It is a rarity in any lifetime to discover our deepest passions, to define a great purpose that would fill our spirits with boundless joy. It is rarer still that, once this discovery is made, you would not only have the vision to know what will fulfill you, but also have the strength of character required to pursue what you love.

To pursue, achieve, and enjoy *a life of passion* will require that you have:

- the *Vision* to recognize what fuels your passion;
- the *Belief* in yourself and ability to prosper;
- the *Courage* to step forward in spite of any fear or opposition;
- the *Discipline* to maintain the daily habits of those who have succeeded before you and allow yourself to be mentored by them; and,
- the *Focus* to concentrate on only those activities that move you closer to your goal, so that you are not merely busy with your activities, but productive.

Will you resolve, right now, to **define your goals**? Will you clarify your mission so that your every action is suffused with a burning desire, one which cannot be easily dissuaded by the challenges our world provides?

Will you resolve, right now, to **master your emotions**? Will you turn your cheek to pessimism; see opportunity where others see disaster; see the blessing disguised as tragedy; laugh in the face of defeat; and use every setback as a challenge to fuel your fire?

Will you resolve, right now, to **enhance your relationships**? To nurture the greatest reward of our human experience—our connection with others whom we love, respect and admire? To lay claim that you were the most devoted and faithful person to your dearest love, a model of integrity and encouragement to your children, an unyielding foundation of support to your most cherished friends?

Will you resolve, right now, to **master your finances**? Will you decide to reject any beliefs that may limit you from a lucrative financial destiny? Will you live a life that attracts abundance and provides the material resources to fully pursue your greatest dreams?

Will you resolve, right now, to **enjoy the life you have through balance**? Will you recognize that your happiness is not found at the end of the journey, but rather along the pathway to achieving your goals?

Will you resolve, right now, to **make a contribution** in this world, to ensure that your life has stood for something inviolate and everlasting? Will you turn your greatest sorrows into a platform for good? Whether it is in saving a life, saving a nation, or raising a child with love, will you do something magnificent for generations to come?

You are embarking on the greatest adventure of your life. You will face challenges you cannot foresee and reap rewards you cannot imagine. Should others around you speak only in doubt, you must act in confidence. Should others around you offer only rejection, you must persist until accepted. Should others falter under the weight of disappointment, you must press on until victorious. Should others find that their passions cool, you must fan the flames of yours.

It is only time that separates the world from learning what we already know to be true: *that within you awaits such great works of beauty; you need only the courage to reveal them.* The time has now come for you to share your greatness with the world. We leave you with this: you have, and can develop, every skill and talent required to excel at your chosen craft and unleash the passion within you.

You are capable of great things. **Now … *go do them!***
With love, respect and admiration for you during your quest,

The POWER WITHIN

Notes

Notes

Notes

Notes

Notes

Notes